MW00446603

Hemingway
and
Bimini

The Birth of Sport Fishing at
"The End of the World"

Ashley Oliphant, Ph.D.

Pineapple Press, Inc.
Sarasota, Florida

Copyright © 2017 Ashley Oliphant

All rights reserved. No part of this book may be reproduced in any form or by any means, electronic or mechanical, including photocopying, recording, or by any information storage and retrieval system, without permission in writing from the publisher.

Inquiries should be addressed to:
Pineapple Press, Inc.
P.O. Box 3889
Sarasota, Florida 34230

www.pineapplepress.com

Cataloging-in-Publication Data is available from the Library of Congress
ISBN 978-1-56164-971-6 (paperback)
ISBN 978-1-56164-979-2 (eBook)

First Edition
10 9 8 7 6 5 4 3 2 1

Design by Modern Alchemy LLC
Printed and bound in the USA

Contents

Dedication:

To my Heavenly Father — for designing a place like Bimini with beauty that exceeds the bounds of human imagination and for gifting me with the privilege of telling her remarkable story.

And to my earthly father — for taking his little girl fishing.

There is "no life except in and on the water" in Bimini.

— Hemingway in a letter to Jane Mason, June 3, 1935

Preface

I REMEMBER THE MOMENT with surprising clarity. It was 1994, and I was a 16-year-old sitting on a South Carolina beach during a family vacation with a fresh, new copy of Ernest Hemingway's *The Old Man and the Sea* in my lap. Reading a short fishing book at the coast seemed like the logical thing to do. The plan on this early morning was to read just a few pages — my first by the author whose image vaguely registered in my mind — and then take a walk or maybe a swim. At lunchtime, I turned the very last page of the novella. I looked out at the whitecaps on the ocean, realizing two things, the first of which was that I was as thoroughly sunburned as a girl could be. Secondly, with a maturity I did not know I yet possessed, I recognized that something profoundly special had just transpired.

As a reader with a little more than 20 years of distance from that day and one who still thinks *The Old Man and the Sea* is the most magnificent piece of fiction penned in the 20th century, I can identify that beach morning as the point at which I contracted the Hemingway bug, an affliction I have happily tolerated into my career as an

English professor. While I like Hemingway's early writing about the modern condition — *In Our Time* (1925), *The Sun Also Rises* (1926), and *A Farewell to Arms* (1929) — I am transfixed by the magic of his craftsmanship once he turned his focus to the sea in *To Have and Have Not* (1937), *The Old Man and the Sea* (1952), and *Islands in the Stream* (1970). The transition Hemingway made in these texts is very clear: he shifted his focus to *place* and allowed the locales of his fiction to exist as main characters, first in Key West for the adventures of Harry Morgan, then to Cuba in narrating Santiago's miraculous journey, and finally to Bimini for Thomas Hudson's tale.

When I was a very green doctoral student at the University of North Carolina at Greensboro, the concept of place in Hemingway's fiction was weighing heavily on my critical mind. In a 2004 presentation titled "The Keys Are the Key: A Defense of the Narrative Structure of Hemingway's *To Have and Have Not*" at the 11ᵗʰ Biennial International Ernest Hemingway Conference in Key West, Florida, I claimed that to fully understand this underappreciated novel, it is essential for the reader to have a full conception (preferably one informed by firsthand experience) of the nature of time and space and indeed general life on the island — not any island, but this one in particular. My assertion hinged upon the concept of Key West as a *liminal space*, a fancy term for the idea that boundaries in the tropics are in a constant state of ambiguity, and the normal structures that one expects from mainland life simply do not apply. It was a gutsy argument to posit, especially considering some of the published critics my little paper took to task were likely in the audience. Looking back on that terrifying but exhilarating day, I am so thankful for the courage to deliver my true opinion. It seems now that a little more than a decade of living, reading, and thinking has brought me full circle, and I find myself a seasoned teacher and a longtime Hemingway reader coming back around to the same argument — this time in book form. *Islands in the Stream* is married to Bimini just as *To Have and Have*

Not is wedded to Key West. As much as I have read about Bimini over the years and as often as I have lost myself in the stunning pictures of the tiny island, I did not really understand the novel and where Hemingway might have eventually taken it if the end had not come too soon in 1961 — that is until Bimini became part of my consciousness in 2016. I hope with this project to paint a picture of Bimini for the reader who never gets the opportunity to experience firsthand "the end of the world," as Hemingway called it (Baker 348).

The *End of the World Bar* in Alice Town is named for Hemingway's famous description of the island.

Dozens of academics and Hemingway contemporaries — from mere acquaintances to dear friends — have written little bits about the author's incredible Bimini days, but nobody to date has ever undertaken and published a complete guide on the subject. We will begin with a very quick look at the unbelievably rich history of the island. From there we will jump feetfirst into the early 1920s, when it was revealed to the world that Bimini was the very best place on the planet to wet a line. Though other priorities intervened and it took him a few years to join the party, Hemingway eventually boarded his beloved *Pilar* and headed northeast from Key West to see what the fuss was all about. With the most skilled anglers in the burgeoning sport of big-game fishing all convened in the same place for three summers, the much-needed International Game Fish Association, still the world's ultimate authority on fishing records and sportsmanship, came into being with Hemingway's guidance and support. A close examination of his ideas about sportsmanship and fair play within the arena of saltwater angling and his superlative fishing adventures around the westernmost Bahamian isle provide the interested scholar with unexpected dimensions to the Hemingway portrait that deserve attention and analysis. Discussion will concentrate specifically on the author's progressive conservationist views several decades before the environmental movement began and his egalitarian ideas about his contemporary female counterparts in the big-game fishing world at the point in time when this hobby was evolving into organized sport.

All of this knowledge sets up the largest questions of the book: why did Hemingway never establish roots and live on the island (even though friend Michael Lerner essentially gave him land) and more importantly, why did he never return after 1937, according to all scholars in the field? For the answers, we will look to the correspondence catalogued in the Hemingway Collection at the John F. Kennedy Presidential Library in Boston and the American Museum of Natural History Library in New York. Attention will then turn to the question of the Bimini land on the King's Highway that Hemingway owned but never used and an examination of the factors likely shaping his decisions. The concluding chapter will analyze his legacy on the island and the impact of those formidable summers in the 1930s whose glory still lives on in the inconceivable stories and iconic photographs of men, women, and fish.

A significant amount of evidence in this book will be gleaned from personal interviews conducted with native Biminites, many of whom have been intimately involved in the preservation of the island's history and some of whom knew Hemingway. One Hemingway family member also contributed evidence to this volume via personal interview. Field research that incorporates personal narratives is always tricky, but this is especially true for my particular project. Exploring the oral tradition related to Hemingway's fishing on Bimini is both amusing and maddening due to the layered nature of narratives. The scholar determined to discern the "truth" will likely wind up beating his or her head against a wall. First, the fishing stories told about Hemingway are filtered through tropical island storytellers, narrators who are notorious for using the kernel of a true event as a springboard for much more fanciful tales that evolve with sometimes increasing embellishments as the years pass and the audiences change. The geography of the Bahamas is part of the underlying reason. Islands are transient places where the population rises and recedes as the ships come and go on the tide. Additionally, *island time* is not just a quirky concept for people on vacation to joke about. Island people really do live on their own terms and timetables. Technology encroaches at a different pace on the island, too, allowing communal activities like storytelling to remain at the center of social gatherings a lot longer than they would on the mainland.

Further complicating matters is that these Bimini stories are often about fishing, and fishing accounts are notoriously exaggerated, with speakers taking enormous liberties for the sake of spinning a good yarn. In fact, it can be argued that one listening to a fishing story actually presumes the speaker will fill in less exciting parts of the narrative with new details, even if they might not be totally true. Another difficulty is these narratives are being told about Ernest Hemingway, one of the most legendary figures of the 20th century and certainly the most notable literary celebrity of the age. Any time history is celebrated, particularly when the figure being lauded is central to the identity of a place, there will be as many versions of the corresponding stories as there were participants. It seems everybody who ever knew Hemingway (from the faithful and close friends to people who may have met him one time) have published their stories or given interviews. If every person who ever knew you gave an interview about their interactions with and opinions of you, the variations would likely be wild, too. It is only fitting that Hemingway himself was known to take creative license when recounting events. In talking about the author's penchant for narrative enrichment, Gregory Hemingway wrote in *Papa: A Personal Memoir*, "My father had a tendency to improve on even the best of real stories" (29). My guess is that the nature of island storytelling is what drew Hemingway to the tropical locales he favored and what kept him entertained long enough to stay a while. The stories are the reason island people and tropical life are so curious. As a creative soul, I think he would have been fed by Bimini, its people, and its storytelling. Anyone who understands the nature of oral narrative will appreciate ornamentation rather than discourage it. Without at least a touch of enhancement, the stories become stagnant and the history loses a bit of its luster. Instead of struggling to reconcile differences of opinion and dates among various speakers, it is best for the researcher to appreciate the stories for what they are and really focus on the mastery of the speaker's delivery. Getting one's shorts in a twist will not resolve the contradictions anyway.

Being a part of Hemingway studies for the past 15 years and writing a dissertation about the author made me think I had a complete grasp on who he was as a man and what he hoped to achieve as an author. While I am generally of the opinion that what readers really need to know about Hemingway's writing can be found in the text, my research for this project has revealed important biographical details about Hemingway as a *sportsman* that have broadened my understanding of his work in important ways. Though many critics contend Hemingway put all of his life in his books, I have come to believe that assertion no longer fits. I have discovered a Hemingway dimension — a very likeable one — that I had never previously noticed. His ideas about fairness, equity, and honest gamesmanship blindsided me in many ways. Drawing additionally on fresh archival work at the International Game Fish Association Museum and Library in Dania Beach, Florida, the aim of this book is to capture this new dimension to the Hemingway portrait and contribute to the ongoing literary conversation about one of the most interesting writers who ever lived.

My eyes are wide open to the realities of Hemingway's complicated perspective, which was certainly a product of his modernist ethos. The contemporary scholar's inability to look past the unsavory aspects of the modern worldview (with its sometimes anti-Semitic, racist, and chauvinistic undertones) and those who insist upon judging writers from the early part of the 20th century through the lens of 21st-century expectations will miss the quite unexpected and progressive aspects found within Hemingway's remarks about sport fishing. The truth of the matter is that such readers would likely never choose to explore the secondary texts (many of which we will cover) where this fertile ground for study resides.

I decided to tackle this book because I am intrigued by Hemingway's writing, I want other readers to discover his work, I like to fish, and Bimini is my idea of paradise. It is as simple as that. Toiling over this manuscript late at night, I have often thought Hemingway would be pleased someone set out to write a book that captures this perfect snapshot in time, and considering all the grief he has been given for his treatment of women (both in life and in the creative realm), I bet he would think it is a hoot that a woman signed up for the job. I am firmly in favor of country singer Billy Currington's life philosophy: "A bad day of fishin[g] beats a good day of anything else." Join me as we travel back in time to relive some of the best fishing days the world has ever known.

Every sailor's son
Is taught when they are young
That the pull of the moon lingers on
Something we can't escape
From Bimini 'round the Cape
Mix in the wind and the sea and sing along.

— Jimmy Buffett, "Tides"

I
A Brief History of Bimini:
Beginnings to 1933

AN ISLAND of such unparalleled natural splendor must have a great backstory, and Bimini's does not disappoint. As one of the more than 700 islands of the Bahamas and the westernmost island in the chain, Bimini is made up of about 10 square miles of terrain. Charles M. Oliver explains in *Ernest Hemingway A to Z*, "The North Bimini Islands are located about 60 miles [approximately 45 nautical miles] due east of Miami and are made up of North and South Bimini, the North Island four miles long and about 300 yards wide for most of its length" (26). The East Bimini landmass wraps around to form the island's idyllic harbor. Because Bimini is actually made up of a chain of islands, the proper way to reference the area is "The Biminis." However, for the sake of brevity, the singular terms "Bimini" or "the island" will be used throughout this work. Bimini's location — at the gate of the New World and on the oceanic highway back to Europe — has historically made it a magnet for the best and worst the sea has to offer, a veritable playground for opportunists, both noble and not.

An aerial view of Bimini in 1936.

During his first summer in Bimini, Hemingway sent friend Sara Murphy a letter dated July 10, 1935, characterizing the magic of the island in his perfectly succinct style: "You would love this place Sara. It's in the middle of the Gulf Stream and every breeze is a cool one. The water is so clear you think you will strike bottom when you have 10 fathoms under your keel. There is every kind of fish [. . .]. There is a pretty good hotel and we have a room there now because there have been rain squalls at night lately so I [can't] sleep on the roof of the boat. That's not a very nautical term but a fine cool place to sleep" (Hendrickson 328). In about 100 words, Hemingway captured the stunning beauty, bounty, and seclusion of the island, all while conveying to Murphy the wildness of his existence there, fishing all day in the blazing tropical sun and sleeping exposed at night on top of his boat when the weather allowed.

The famous clear waters of Bimini are a product of the geology and geography of the Bahamas. Michael Craton reveals in *A History of the Bahamas* that because the string of islands is mostly flat and as a result of the porous nature of Bimini's rocks, it has no rivers or rivulets (11). These factors combine to produce waters that "are the clearest in the world. The ocean floor can be seen, as through crystal, in 60 feet of water" (13). As a first-time visitor to the island, I was in disbelief when I dipped my toes in those delightfully warm waters and saw with clarity various sea creatures, some of which were quite a distance away.

Even people who have traveled extensively in the Caribbean will be mesmerized by the clarity of Bimini's ocean water.

Once Hemingway established himself as a bona fide working author (probably after the commercial success of *The Sun Also Rises* in 1926) and certainly the next year after he divorced his first wife Hadley and married Pauline (from the extraordinarily wealthy Pfeiffer pharmaceutical family — the same one that funded the original construction of the college campus where I teach), his financial prospects for travel were vastly expanded. With such grand options at his disposal, it is fascinating to consider the locales where he decided to stay a spell. The three tropical locations — Key West, Cuba, and

Bimini — share obvious parallels. All three islands offer some of the best weather conditions on the planet. In Bimini, a 90-degree day is a rarity, and the lowest temperature on record is 30 degrees. Even though Key West and Cuba tend to endure more heat and humidity than Bimini, the record lows are very similar: 41 degrees for Key West and 33 degrees for Cuba. The favorable climes (especially for fishing) of all three locations obviously suited Hemingway's tastes, but even more than that, I speculate that Key West, Cuba, and Bimini fed his imagination with their outlandishly rich histories.

All three islands also offered a sense of anonymity, despite the fact that he was obviously a famous face. Multiple aspects of his biography and his fiction suggest he genuinely enjoyed mixing with locals and hearing what they had to say. In Key West (at least in the beginning), Bimini, and Cuba, he was allowed by the residents to blend in, leave all pretension on the mainland and just be himself. In describing his life in the late 1940s in Cuba to the magazine *Holiday*, Hemingway wrote when people ask why one might live on that island, you might say it was because "you only have to put shoes on when you come into town," and you have the freedom to "plug the bell in the party-line telephone with paper so that you won't have to answer" if you are not in the mood ("The Great Blue River" 61). Writers of fiction require a place that nourishes their creative appetite but can simultaneously provide a place of refuge to work uninterrupted. The choices Hemingway made about where to live during his writing years clearly indicate he was seeking a place that would provide the elusory combination of stimulating activity and sacred solitude.

This chapter will explore the historical highlights that likely piqued Hemingway's interest and compelled him to use Bimini as the canvas for a major piece of work that would be included in his vision for a sea trilogy, a project he unfortunately never had the chance to complete. He was clearly searching for a refuge, and Bimini in the 1930s was perfectly suited to his temperament and his sporting appetite. His trips there do not necessarily mean he was looking to escape, as Leicester Hemingway, the author's brother, pointed out in an interview with Bimini historian Ashley Saunders in his tremendously important *History of Bimini* series: While "Bimini is a place where a lot of people come to duck and hide," Hemingway "came to explore and for the adventure, but not to hide out" (*Volume 1*, 144). As a larger-than-life character, he needed a small town that appreciated and could accommodate gregarious personalities. As we will see, Hemingway caused some commotion in Bimini, likely because he knew he had found a tolerant place full of people who would welcome the humor of his antics. Considering, too, how much he would write about the ocean in the following years, it is obvious he also came to the island to study. Every person he met and every experience he enjoyed was fully absorbed and mentally catalogued for later.

While Hemingway is the most notable extended visitor to the island, he was just one among many. Beginning in the 15th century, Bimini hosted some of the world's most compelling historical figures, including Christopher Columbus, Juan Ponce de León, Blackbeard, Zane Grey, Al Capone, Howard Hughes, Dr. Martin Luther King, Jr., and Jimmy Buffett, and it has served as the backdrop for a remarkable number of significant events. An early Biminite's opinion of the island would depend entirely on his or her position in the economy of the time. If you were a pirate or an explorer, Bimini was a playground with matchless beauty and endless possibility. If you were a Lucayan native or an imported slave, Bimini looked more like the gates of hell from your vantage point. To obtain the full scope of the island's history, the reader must imagine people and events that even the most respected ancient scholars cannot speak about with certainty. Bimini's dramatic story begins thousands of years *before* Columbus ever set foot on Bahamian sand.

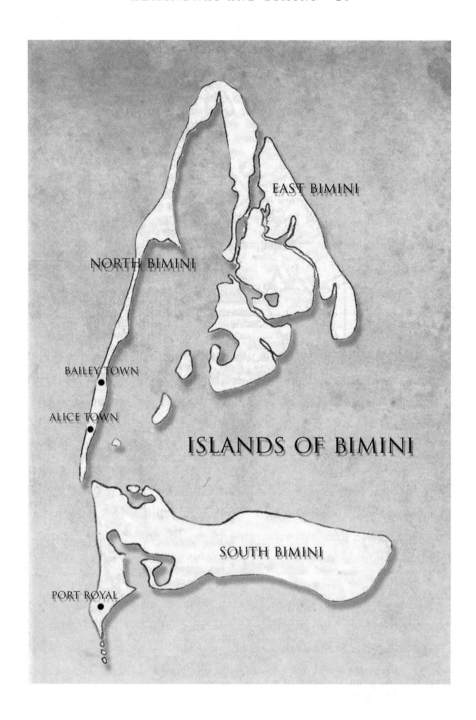

The Lost City of Atlantis

The earliest visitors to the Bahamas — whoever they were — experienced a landscape that looked quite different from the islands we visit today. Craton explains the current composition of the Bahamas is "the result of changes brought about by the most recent Ice Age, the Wisconsin, which is believed to have occurred between 64,000 and 11,000 years ago," a time when "the water level was probably 250 feet lower than it is" now (15); therefore, the landmass above the water in Bimini was much larger. This time frame sets up an interesting possibility for the famed Lost City of Atlantis. In his dialogues *Critias* and *Timaeus*, ancient Greek philosopher and mathematician Plato refers to Atlantis as an advanced, powerful and wealthy civilization that sank into the ocean around 10,000 BCE. Plato admits he received the narrative about the legend third-hand (through his grandfather, a friend, and then a priest). Situated beyond the Pillars of Hercules (near the Strait of Gibraltar), Atlantis was said to be a landmass larger than Africa and Asia put together. The vast majority of scholars of ancient philosophy who analyze Plato's dialogues assert this story is just that — a made-up tale to demonstrate a larger point about society. Considering Plato's dialogues refer to the gods inhabiting Atlantis, the opinion of the philosophy experts that it was simply a mythical place seems prudent. Even so, the legend never died, and for centuries mariners have invested resources and set out on expeditions to search for the real Atlantis. Interestingly enough, in the 20th century the investigation shifted to Bimini when large underwater rock formations were discovered just off the island's coast. These rocks are now known as "Bimini Road" and have been the subject of documentaries by National Geographic and The History Channel, in addition to being a favorite diving location for tourists. It is hard to believe, but the rock formations are "completely identical in design to known harbor [. . .] installations submerged in the Mediterranean, which indicates they were built at the same period, by the same sea-faring people" (Saunders, *Volume 1*, 49). Having seen the Bimini Road with my own eyes from above the water and having studied many of the published texts relating to it, I can say the rocks definitely look man-made. You can find Atlantis stories as wild as you want them — including narrative strains involving ancient intervention from aliens who traveled from the Pleiades. While investigating the possible theories of Atlantis's origins is fascinating work, tread carefully as part of the lost city's story includes psychic predictions that are not always labeled as such in the literature, and the innocent reader can quickly get off track from legitimate scientific inquiry and into dark spiritual territory. No matter whether you believe Atlantis was a real civilization, there is no question that the mysterious rocks that pepper the Bimini coastline add to the island's appeal.

Bimini Road: It is just offshore near the Hilton and the Resorts World Bimini cruise ship dock. You can only see it by boat. The rock formation is in the vicinity of the Three Sisters Rock. It is parallel to shore from the Hilton's Paradise Beach.

The First Natives and Contact

In *Liberties Lost: Caribbean Indigenous Societies and Slave Systems*, Hilary Beckles and Verene A. Shepherd explain the latest anthropological and archaeological research suggests "prehistoric human development" existed on the American continent millions of years ago instead of 25,000 years ago, as scholars who ascribe to landbridge theory have argued (3). The first native group that moved into the Bahamas was the Ciboney (alternately spelled "Siboney"), a tribe later overtaken and enslaved by the invading Lucayans. The consensus among scholars seems to be that the Ciboneys came from South America. Native bands in the Caribbean were constantly moving from island to island and encountering one another. While a great deal is known about the history of the Lucayans, information about the Ciboneys is much more sporadic. Saunders credits the Lucayans with giving Bimini its name (*Volume 2*, 2). We do know the Lucayans were in Bimini when Columbus made his way into the Bahamas in the 15th century.

The Bahamas issued this stamp in 1992 to commemorate the landing of Christopher Columbus. The tragic irony of the image is that the natives depicted in it were all carried into slavery or killed within a few years after contact.

By the time we reach Columbus's landing in 1492, details about Bimini and its inhabitants are revealed with more certainty because the "discovery" led to the first written history of the land. Some say the place where Columbus landed on present-day San Salvador Island was called Watling's, though there has been some disagreement on this issue amongst published scholars. Craton asserts the landing "was almost certainly somewhere in Fernández or Long Bay, Watling's [. . .] close to the Indian village site where, on July 4, 1983 Charles Hoffman's archeological crew uncovered unique Spanish trade artifacts in conjunction with Lucayan remains" (34). Columbus only stayed in the Bahamas for two weeks, but the impact of his landing was massive and swift for the world of trade, for the Spanish realm, and for the coming settlement of the New World. Most important, though, was the effect of Columbus's voyage on the lives of the Lucayans. We all remember from history class that as a shameless self-promoter, Columbus marched across the globe with his chest puffed out, acting with complete disregard for the people he encountered. In a letter about his first voyage to King Ferdinand and Queen Isabella of Spain, the monarchs who funded his journey, he admitted, "As soon as I arrived in the Indies, in the first island which I found, I took by force some of the natives" (Belasco and Johnson 71). In the same letter, he generalized about "the people of this island [Juana/ Cuba] and of all the other islands which I have found" (70). Reading his description of the natives makes one question why Americans still celebrate Columbus Day:

> [T]hey are so guileless and so generous with all that they
> possess, that no one would believe it who has not seen it.
> They refuse nothing that they possess, if it be asked of them;
> on the contrary, they invite any one to share it and display as
> much love as if they would give their hearts. They are con-

tent with whatever trifle of whatever kind it may be that is given to them, whether it be of value or valueless. I forbade that they should be given things so worthless as fragments of broken crockery, scraps of broken glass and ends of straps, although when they were able to get them, they fancied that they possessed the best jewel in the world. (70)

We also know from the history books that the Spanish did not set up shop in the Bahamas and instead kept searching for their real goal: gold and silver deposits that would bring the Crown even more wealth. They went on to other islands and found their prize, realizing then that they would need a lot of help to mine it. They remembered the Lucayan natives from the Bahamas and went back. It is a chilling thought, but historians believe that "between 1500 and 1520 the entire population of the Bahamas, probably about 20,000 Lucayans, was carried off" into slavery (Craton 39). Just 28 years removed from first contact with European explorers, all the Lucayans were gone, and the abuses they faced in their removal and transport were horrific. The only thing the Bahamas had that the Spanish wanted was its human capital, so they did not establish a permanent colony.

The Famous Fountain of Youth

As if the search for the mysterious Atlantis in Bimini was not enough, the island was identified by Spanish mariner Ponce de León as a possible site of the Fountain of Youth. The Spanish got wind of a Lucayan legend about a healing spring in Bimini with supernatural powers, and as world history proves, if the Spanish wanted something, they would do anything to attain it. Ponce de León traveled with Columbus on his second voyage to Hispaniola in 1493; once they returned to Spain, Ponce de León was given a charter by the Spanish crown to explore Florida and the Bahamas, settle in Bimini, and search for the Fountain. He made it to the Bahamas in 1513 to begin his search but did not find the storied spring. While in the Bahamas, he "encountered a single Amerindian, an aged woman on Bimini or Grand Bahama, which he therefore named La Vieja. It is thus ironic that Peter Martyr [an Italian who served as a historian and writer for Spain] associated this voyage with the search for a fountain of youth," which scholars afterward associated with Bimini exclusively (Craton and Saunders *Volume 1*, 56). It is probably impossible to ever know for sure, but if Ponce de León was ever actually in Bimini, he likely did not know it because the area was still uncharted in the 16th century. He was later given the title of Adelantado Don Juan Ponce de León, Governor of the Islands of Bimini and Florida, but he never settled a colony there as his charter required. Faithfully, he tried to make it to Bimini in 1521 to satisfy the requirements of the charter, but on the way he made a stop in Florida and was fatally wounded by the natives there.

The island's early connections to the search for the elusive spring have been commemorated in a number of ways. Rumrunner Bruce Bethel, who will factor prominently in the Bimini story later in this chapter, actually opened a bar and cabaret on the island called the Fountain of Youth. Near the airport on South Bimini, a freshwater well has been labeled by the islanders as the Fountain of Youth to acknowledge the interest the legend has brought to their culture. Coincidentally, Hemingway's brother, Leicester, who lived on Bimini in the last few years before his death in 1982, spent time searching for the Fountain of Youth on the island. When I was in Bimini in 2016, I kept my eyes peeled, but regrettably no healing spring revealed itself to me.

The years following the Fountain of Youth search were marked by multiple attempts at settlement, the first official one of which was established by Englishman William Sayle in 1646. Twenty years later, the first plantations (and thus the first slaves) were introduced into the established economy of the islands (Saunders *Volume 1*, 6), an economy that would continue to be supported by slave labor for more than 200 years. Those readers who faithfully completed their history homework are aware of the next cast of raucous characters waiting to invade this delightful island.

"The Golden Age of Piracy" Dawns in the Bahamas

The historical synopsis of any good nautical town is incomplete without a spirited pirate tale. Bahamians have more than a story or two to share because their stretch of little islands became pirate central from the late 1600s into the 1700s. Before then (around the 1660s), Port Royal, Jamaica, had been the hub of pirate activity. Luckily for the Jamaicans, effective pirate policing and natural disasters such as a major earthquake forced the pirates to settle elsewhere (Butler 11). Being the opportunists that they were, the pirates sought a new location with lax governmental oversight and a favorable physical landscape. New Providence, Bahamas, approximately 112 nautical miles from Bimini, turned out to be the hapless winner.

The location of the Bahamas in general made it exceptionally appealing as Europeans began to explore the New World and eventually to set up a trading route. The positioning of Bimini in particular, considering that it is the last scenic little stop before landing in North America or continuing on to the south, increased the level of seafaring activity it experienced compared to the other Bahamian islands (New Providence excluded). Robert E. Lee explains in the superb *Blackbeard the Pirate: A Reappraisal of His Life and Times*, "Many of the ablest and best-known pirates used [New Providence Island] as their base of operations. The Atlantic Ocean has, in that region, currents, shoals, and surfs that make navigation extremely hazardous, particularly for large merchant ships. The small craft generally used by pirates, however, could be navigated safely through the treacherous waters" (9–10). The ability to traverse these dangerous seas also made it possible for pirates and all of the salty characters they brought with them to hide in the Bahamas when the need arose, as it surely did with great frequency.

Lee characterizes New Providence (which includes the national capital of Nassau) during the Golden Age of Piracy as "nothing more than a mariner's resort, a place where the ordinary sailor or pirate could go for a few days to whoop it up and let off steam" (10). The who's who of the pirate ranks whooped it up in grand style, from "Calico Jack" Rackham, Charles Vane, and Benjamin Hornigold to Mary Read and Anne Bonney, two notorious female pirates who disguised their identities to sail the high seas. Most interesting, of course, is the fact that the great Blackbeard called the Bahamas home from the late 1600s to 1717, though he was obviously in and out of town on "business" quite a lot. Blackbeard went off the radar in 1717, resurfacing in Charleston, South Carolina, for his famous blockade of that port city. In my overactive imagination, the legends about pirate booty being buried in Bimini are true, and there are chests full of jewels waiting to be discovered somewhere on the island. The reader

---

Major Bimini Historical Events: Beginnings to 1933

300 BCE: Plato mentions Atlantis in *Timeaus* and *Critias*

500 A.D. to 1000 CE: Siboneys and Lucayans inhabit Bimini

1492: Columbus lands in the Bahamas

1513: Ponce de León arrives to search for the Fountain of Youth

1521: Ponce de León is killed on the way to Bimini

1650–1730: Golden Age of Piracy

1783: Spain relinquishes the Bahamas to England with Treaty of Paris

1834: Emancipation of slaves in British Empire

1861–65: Blockade-running

1840–1919: Bimini Wrecking

1920–1933: American Prohibition

should also know I had no luck locating pirate treasure when I was in Bimini, though my failure was not from lack of trying.

While most of what is written about piracy in the Bahamas focuses on New Providence, the close physical proximity to the other islands makes it understood that pirates visited all of them with regularity. By 1716, New Providence was the stomping ground of more than 500 pirates ("Pirate Den: New Providence"), and officials across the pond in England began to devise a Hail Mary amnesty plan to end the deviant practice. When Englishman Woodes Rogers pulled into port in Nassau, 200 pirate vessels were anchored and more than 3,000 pirates were in town (Saunders *Volume 2*, 7). Amazingly, the crafty leadership of Rogers, who became the first Royal Governor of the Bahamas, squelched pirate activity in the area by the time The Golden Age closed with the calendar nearing 1730, securing Rogers's place in history as the biggest party pooper of all time.

A shipwreck can be seen on South Bimini near the Bimini Shark Lab live wells.

Slavery, War, Wrecking, and Blockade-Running

A long line of English leaders guided the Bahamas with varying levels of success through the 1700s, and control of the islands changed hands frequently with temporary invasions (including those from the lingering Spanish) all the way through the American Revolution. Spain officially gave up the struggle in 1783, ceding the Bahamas to England after the Treaty of Paris. Despite the changes in leadership, what remained constant in the Bahamas was its plantation culture, and by the 1810s, slavery was at a nasty crescendo in the islands. Craton reveals that in 1831, "there were 12,259 Negroes in the Bahamas, outnumbering the white inhabitants by three to one" (173). It is important to temper the romance of the uncharted island and the swashbuckling adventures that took place in Bimini with the reality that history almost always has a heinous underbelly.

The end of slavery in the Bahamas came sooner (1834) than emancipation for American slaves (1863). Because the plantation was the foundation of Bahamian industry, emancipation brought about total economic collapse. As was the case in post-slavery America, many emancipated Bahamian slaves stayed put, mainly because as the slave masters were planning their exit, their former slaves were gifted with parcels of property that were not especially prosperous for farming (Saunders *Volume 2*, 12). In fact, many of the current families on the island are descended from the population of emancipated slaves. The family names of the early settlers were the same ones visitors in the 21st century encounter in talking to the people of the island: Saunders, Francis, Sherman, Hield, Brady, Weech, Levarity, and Rolle ("Wrecking 1840–1919"). In fact, several members of the Saunders family and one member of the Francis family were interviewed on my first day on the island.

Beginning in the early 1800s, industrious islanders had begun making a living off the carnage left over after unlucky mariners discovered Bimini's coastal hazards firsthand. Disagreement among sources exists about when the first families settled the island for the purpose of *wrecking* in the late 1840s. Paul Albury claims in *The Story of the Bahamas* that South Bimini was used mostly for farming and North Bimini for settlement around this time. However, "when wrecking increased tremendously toward the middle of the nineteenth century, some of the wreckers decided it would be better to live close to the scene of their business activities" (246–7). Bimini "had been uninhabited before 1847, when Alice Town was laid out and settled" as a citrus grove serving United States customers (Craton and Saunders *Volume 1*, 142). When that business plan did not come to fruition, wrecking served as a pretty handy alternative plan.

The geography of North Bimini, with its prominent ridge overlooking the splendor of the Gulf Stream — the same promontory on which the land Mike Lerner gave Hemingway sits today — made the perfect vantage point. Wrecking was such a vital component of the island's economy that a wrecking tower was built on North Bimini to aid the searchers (Saunders *Volume 1*, 69). Sir Michael Checkley, the director of the Bimini Museum, suggested in a personal interview that no information exists about the location of the Bimini wrecking tower because "there is no oral tradition concerning its whereabouts. Only speculation places it along what is now Radio Beach or south of the southern cemetery. This being the case, it must have been constructed in the late 1800s and survived only for a short time." Islanders would climb to the top and simply wait on trouble. Though some folktales exist that suggest unfortunate ships may have been helped into wrecking by various means, no firm evidence grounds such claims. Bimini's wrecking past provides yet another of those hilarious historical moments that I would pay good money to go back in time and witness. Not surprisingly, however, wrecking was an industry with a very limited window of opportunity; shortly after the turn of the century, it was gone.

The southern tip of North Bimini looking toward South Bimini. Historians think the Bimini wrecking tower could have been located anywhere from this point around to Radio Beach (where Mike Lerner's Anchorage was later built).

The American Civil War (1861–1865) brought about another brief flurry of economic activity as blockade-running exploded in the Bahamas. Thelma Peters, in the introductory paragraph of "Blockade-Running in the Bahamas During the Civil War," classifies the effect of this new profession on the island as "electrifying," writing that Nassau "with an ordinarily poor and indifferent population, became overnight the host to a reckless, wealthy and extravagant crowd of men from many nations and many ranks" (16). For a point of reference, consider the scoundrel Rhett Butler from Margaret Mitchell's *Gone with the Wind*, a man who joined the company of those Peters describes, much to the chagrin of polite society in Atlanta. The idea of the Bahamas suddenly becoming eaten up with blockade-runners adds yet another enticing layer to its character.

Prohibition and Rum-Running

A plethora of additional industries arose and then faded in Bimini from the late 1800s through the early 1900s, including sponging, turtling, conch harvesting, and shelling. Considering the previous pattern of its history, it was only a matter of time before the next untoward industry in Bimini arose. Saunders identifies 1919 as a pivotal turning point for Bimini because that was when "Albert Burns 'Pappy' Chalk began scheduled airline flights to Bimini from Miami, Florida in his single-engine plane, the United States Congress passed the Volstead Prohibition Act over President Woodrow Wilson's veto, and construction was started on the Bimini Bay Rod and Gun Club [the island's first hotel]" (*Volume 1*, 94). Businessmen who participated in rum-running profited profoundly from American Prohibition, which began in 1920 and ran all the way through 1933. Again, because of the island's position just off the American coast, it became a natu-

The SS *Sapona* (in about 1931) looked like a jolly place for a floating nightclub.

ral outpost for smuggling. In keeping with its tradition of attracting ruffians, Bimini was a known destination for gangsters such as Al Capone, who came to town to meet with liquor dealers and negotiate major sales.

This new economic opportunity could not have come at a better time for the island, which at that time was in a depression. In "Bimini, Bahamas: Hemingway's Island in the Stream," Jane Day claims, "During Prohibition the island had boomed with the rum-running trade. Thousands of cases of liquor had been sold and shipped on speed boats back to Florida. As a British Colony, this trade was completely legal [. . .] and the government benefited as well as the citizenry" (6). Evidence of the rum-running era can still be seen on the horizon off Bimini, as the dilapidated remains of the concrete ship SS *Sapona* jut out of the water. Bethel, the famous Bahamian rumrunner mentioned earlier, purchased the ship in 1924 and intended to use it as a "floating liquor warehouse" (Bennett). Unfortunately for Bethel, as the ship was being towed to Bimini, it wrecked in the shallow

The SS *Sapona* wreckage today is only a hollow shell of the ship she used to be. Her profile on the horizon serves as a navigational beacon for fishermen.

waters. Bethel tried to amend his plan and "turn the *Sapona* into a nightclub, an attraction that would've no doubt lured many a drink-starved American across the scant 53 miles of open water separating South Florida and the Bimini Islands" (Bennett). To his dismay, the great hurricane of 1926 thrashed the wrecked *Sapona* and thwarted that plan. Merrily, the *Sapona's* memory lives on as she greets the boatmen coming to and from Bimini each day.

In his "Fishing at Bimini" chapter originally published in Eugene V. Connett III's 1935 book called *American Big Game Fishing*, Selwyn Kip Farrington, Jr., the longtime saltwater editor for *Field & Stream*, prolific writer of all things fishing and a master angler, provided all the specifics a fisherman would need to know on the island. He wrote, "Now that the rum running is over, your party should be safe when evening fishing from being run down by rum runners, Florida bound, with a heavy load and no lights" (118). He also predicted an improvement in harbor fishing due to the reduced boat traffic. Van Campen Heilner, the big-game fisherman who is credited with discovering Bimini's sporting potential, explained in his book *Salt Water Fishing* (originally published in 1937) that after the 1926 hurricane wiped out the rumrunners' storage boats at Gun Key, they "moved up to Bimini and a safe harbor" (126). He described Bimini in those days as "very colorful" but "never a dive and never a disturbance," mainly because the rumrunners, "the actual men who ran the liquor into the States, and who were the only ones breaking the law, never stayed at Bimini. They crossed from Miami during the night, loaded up during the day and went back during that late afternoon or night" (132–133). American Prohibition provided only a 13-year window for profitability, and by 1933, Biminites were again in need of a new livelihood. Yet again, the next opportunity arrived right on time. Pretty much the minute American Prohibition ended in 1933, word got out that Bimini's waters were absolutely full of giant game fish. Big-game fishermen descended on the island, creating a new hospitality-based economy designed to serve those from around the world who heard about the island's abundant sporting opportunities.

◆

Even though this historical synopsis is abbreviated, the reader can see the tiny island of Bimini has witnessed more than its fair share of important history. Rich history translates to rich cultural heritage, the heartbeat that gives all interesting locations their specific personalities. The totality of Bimini's charm, however, is much more than the sum of its historical events and its illustrious visitors. This chapter pointed out earlier that Hemingway was drawn to islands in the final three decades of his life. His focus on writing required a regimented schedule; daily dedication to the craft is the only way great books are produced. If Key West, Bimini, and Cuba were his selections, the relaxed pace of island life and the loose attitude with which islanders regarded constraints such as time and space had to factor into Hemingway's decisions. Any visitor to a true tropical island who can let go

of mainland stress will quickly settle into island time and accept that there is no need to rush because all things will get done in due time. So many people in modern-day cultures have grown accustomed to a GPS-guided, "on-the-grid" existence. In their minds, it should be possible to chart their next moves with precision and to control the outcomes. The islanders' conception of existence is just the opposite. They are most comfortable operating in an arena where the boundaries are blurry and time is indefinite. That Hemingway consecutively chose three islands suggests he was personally attracted to the tropical worldview and the creative fuel that was so abundant in these locations. What a relief those island days must have been for his spirit at a crossroads in world history where pretty much everything was going wrong. It is no coincidence that these islands became the settings for the fiction that would occupy his creative world for so many years.

While Bimini's history must have intrigued Hemingway and the pace of island life clearly suited him, the main reason he decided to crank up his boat and make the trip was the fishing. Hemingway was not part of the first wave of anglers to discover Bimini as a world-class fishing destination, but his buddies were, and their writing about the unprecedented angling events unfolding on the island must have been irresistible to him. It just took them a few years to effectively twist his arm.

Bimini's delicious slice of the Gulf Stream as seen from a fishing boat.

How those babies can leap! You can close your eyes and see them
now, thrashing about on the surface, their great swords wagging
from side to side, mouths open, gills slapping, walking on their
tails, or coming out in clean greyhound jumps that sometimes
carry them and all your line out of sight on the horizon. There's
absolutely nothing like it anywhere on earth or in the waters over
earth. It's marvelous, breath-taking, terrific!

— Van Campen Heilner, *Salt Water Fishing*

II

Setting the Stage: How Bimini Became the "Sport Fishing Capital of the World"

THE RISE OF sport fishing in Bimini beginning around the time of World War I was the result of an unbelievable confluence of complex factors. The brief flash of light that was the birth of big-game angling was largely due to the presence of an unimaginably interesting cast of fishing personalities and a series of fishing adventures that, on first reading, seem hard to accept as truth. If I could choose any historical period in which to live, I would want to be on a boat in 1930s Bimini. Simply put, it gets no better than the story about to unfold in the next two chapters. As an added bonus, the unbridled adventures of these formative years were captured by some of the best sporting writers who have ever put pen to paper. The interested reader will find no shortage of masterful accounts of the astounding angling feats carried out by the best anglers of the 20th century on a tiny island of such majesty that there is no doubt God was working overtime with his best palette of colors on the day it was designed.

S. Kip Farrington, Jr.

Why Bimini?

The previous chapter explored the multitude of physical character-istics that make Bimini such a unique place. As the discussion turns to the emergence of big-game fishing in the area, the actual oceanic geography of the island takes center stage. Farrington had more to say about Bimini's particular attributes than any other writer of the time. In his 1937 *Atlantic Game Fishing*, he wrote,

> Approximately two miles off the Great Bahama Bank is a great shelf which drops abruptly from the reef, and there the water reaches a depth of from two to five thousand feet. [...] The Gulf Stream usually flows very fast past these islands; four or five knots is not unusual, and as the water behind

the islands is very shoal, the outgoing tide frequently sweeps a great many of the smaller fish out into the deeper water beyond the shelf, thus providing a rich feeding ground for the big ones outside. The three factors responsible for Bimini's prominence as a fishing center are, to my mind, the great depth of the water, the rapidly moving Gulf Stream current, and the abundance of fish which serve as food for the big fish. (182–83)

The Gulf Stream moves almost four billion cubic feet of water each second, a volume larger than all of the planet's rivers combined ("How Fast is the Gulf Stream?"). The size and length of the warm, fast-moving current are responsible for its healthy population of fish. Mike Rivkin, in the seminal *Big-Game Fishing Headquarters: A History of the IGFA*, writes that the Gulf Stream carries "a collection of pelagic game fish more than 2,500 miles" on a "pelagic highway [. . .] barely a stone's throw from Bimini, itself already home to more than 600 species of marine fish" (102). The observer can actually see the azure waters of the Gulf Stream from the beach, and the angler in a boat can fish those extraordinarily deep warm waters not much farther out to sea than an average fishing pier. The Gulf Stream became an obsession for Hemingway beginning in the early 1930s, and afterward he never seemed to lose his curiosity about it. *A Sea of Change: Ernest Hemingway and the Gulf Stream*, Mark P. Ott's beautifully written account of the connection between the author's writing and fishing, explores the evolution of Hemingway's thinking about the great river from "a space of conquest to a relationship that allowed him to understand it as a place of personal integration and harmony" (x). The Gulf Stream was created as a force with the power to govern the animal kingdom and the humans who seek to comprehend her mysteries.

Notice the dark blue water just off the coast of Radio Beach. The sapphire blue
Gulf Stream can be seen with the naked eye from shore.

Native Biminites obviously knew their waters contained very
big fish. However, Ashley Saunders argues that before the emergence
of big-game fishing on the island, the natives did not pursue these
fish because they had no way of successfully landing them (*Volume
1,* 161). The primitive fishing tackle that existed at the turn of the
century and in the 30 years or so afterward was very expensive, and
almost every tool on the market was woefully inadequate to land a
massive tuna or marlin. Most of these old rods did not even have drag
systems, a reality that makes the early catches of mammoth game fish
even more incredible.

The Main Players Take the Stage

The first non-native to come to Bimini and discover its fishing potential was Van Campen Heilner, a dedicated sportsman who was
inducted into the International Game Fish Association Hall of Fame

in 1998 in its first class. Hemingway himself sang Heilner's praises in the preface he wrote for the 1953 edition of the crucially important *Salt Water Fishing*. Acknowledging the influence of the book and the contributions of Heilner, Hemingway expressed his gratitude for Heilner's book, crediting him as a pioneer who "fished out of Bimini long before most of today's famous fishermen had ever heard the name of that place" (vii). Hemingway lauded the fact that his friend was as happy catching a bonefish as he was with landing "the huge fish for which no labor-saving tackle had yet been devised" (viii). The author's critical appraisal is the first of many examples this study will include of the early big-game innovators writing about each other and for the fishing books of others. There is no room in this book to fully explore the fascinating connections that linked these phenomenal anglers, but it is worth the reader's effort to independently study the intertwined trajectories of these earliest pioneers in the Works Cited list at the end of this work.

Of all the writing to come out of this remarkable era, Heilner's delivers so much value because he documents what it was like to live in Bimini before any other sportsmen discovered it. Despite his family's wealth and his freedom to live anywhere in the world, he chose to rough it on an undeveloped tropical island simply because he fed off the spirit of pure adventure. Even though he first arrived on a yacht in 1920, Heilner set up a fishing camp north of Porgy Bay at Paradise Point and was actually living in a tent (Thornton). In 1924 he built a permanent home, the first concrete house in Bimini (Saunders *Volume 1*, 128). In the first edition of *Salt Water Fishing*, Heilner wrote, "Along about 1920 my search for solitude and quiet led me to the Bahamas. I cruised around through most of them and finally settled on Bimini [. . .]. It was a beautiful island, with more coconut trees than I'd ever seen and the natives were kindly and unspoiled" (123). He was a fierce protector of the untainted nature of the island, and his early writings indicate how much he wanted to preserve

Van Campen Heilner

what he considered to be a very safe haven from the outside world. In those days, Bimini could not even be considered an outpost despite its close proximity to the American mainland. Saunders points out the effects of the 1926 hurricane that were still crippling the island, as "there were no hotel facilities, no docks, no ice, no fresh water, no electricity, no weight-scale, and no fresh bait available" in addition to no restaurants (*Volume 1*, 161–162). With few creature comforts to offer visiting Americans, it is clear travelers like Heilner chose to stay because they were satisfied by the untouched natural beauty of the place. In those early days, Bimini native Nathaniel Saunders, who will figure into the island's story in the next chapter, served as Heilner's fishing guide.

The Bimini Bay Rod and Gun Club opened in 1922 but closed in 1925 due to mismanagement (Saunders, *Volume 1*, 95). The hurricane of 1926 destroyed it. This photograph was taken by Captain Bill Fagen in 1925, one year before the storm. The hotel was located on the southern end of North Bimini.

Perhaps the most likeable of Heilner's characteristics is that he actually uncovered the presence of enormous game fish in Bimini, but he decided to keep quiet about it for a few years to savor the secret. Heilner wrote nonchalantly, "I think it was about 1925 that I discovered there were big marlin off Bimini. I'd suspected it the year before but I wasn't certain" (129). After hooking but not catching his first big marlin in Bimini, he said, "I was torn between my anxiety to tell my friends of my discovery and my selfishness to keep it to myself. And I did the latter. I've been ashamed ever since and this is my apology" (130). Rivkin explains that even with Heilner's considerable angling skills, he continually failed to bring in a big fish before "finally catching a pair of small blue marlin in 1925" (36). While some sources credit other anglers (such as Kip Farrington) with hooking the first blue marlin in Bimini, Heilner should hold the honor in my opinion. Heilner's worry about proclaiming Bimini's fishing promise was warranted. His list of fears illustrates how much he cared for his little island: "Real estate offices would blossom like mushrooms" and nights would be "made hideous with jazz bands and jazzing" (130–131). He made the deliberate decision to keep quiet, catch his bonefish, and go on with his Bimini business. He admitted that he knew the secret of the island would eventually be revealed to the world, and luckily, "it came the right way and the right people came with it. But I think that they, too, caught some of the charm and simplicity of our lovely island and are unanimous in their determination to keep it simple and unspoiled" (131). The friends Heilner finally told about the island turned out to be a who's who of the angling world, and luckily they did recognize "the charm and simplicity" of the island and desired to preserve it as well. Zane Grey, famous novelist, world-class angler, and IGFA Hall of Fame inductee, was among Heilner's invitees. In "Hemingway: A Love Affair with Bimini," the author's grandson, John Patrick Hemingway, reports Grey called Bimini "a sport fisherman's dream come true." The younger Hemingway also credits Grey with "introduc[ing] the well-heeled of the Roaring Twenties to the

Bimini's bay front in 1932. The building to the right was a dance hall and bar built on the water. The structure in the center is Bruce Bethel's Fountain of Youth bar. Both buildings were destroyed by a hurricane.

challenges of catching marlin and sailfish. His books and many world records also played a part in enticing my grandfather to the Keys and eventually to Bimini." Heilner credited Grey with doing "more to publicize the world's greatest marlin centers than anyone else. He's spent his life and his fortune at it" (131). Grey gained notoriety in the angling world by landing the first fish over 1,000 pounds in Tahiti in 1930, though the fish was mauled by sharks. Heilner and his Bimini guests enjoyed the fishing and wisely kept to themselves about it. The 1920s passed quietly enough on the island (with the exception of the hubbub associated with the rum-running trade, which was in full swing) as the anglers who had discovered it kept things low-key and relished their private paradise, a shrewd strategy indeed.

The pace of the fishing life on the island changed dramatically in the 1930s as the movers and shakers in what was then the expanding fellowship of sport fishermen came to town. The swift expansion in Bimini was contextualized by Florida journalist Erl Roman in a 1938 edition of *Motor Boating* magazine: "Just a few short years ago, a half-dozen fishing cruisers at the Bimini docks constituted a crowd. Today you will find 50 or more of the world's finest fishing crafts in the water" (19). Without question, the most important invitee to the Heilner fishing camp was Michael Lerner, a figure who turned out to be the most influential player in the development of big-game fishing worldwide. A wildly successful New York businessman and co-founder of the Lerner Shops that eventually became the massive retail chain New York & Company, he first came to the island in 1933 with his lovely wife Helen, a skilled angler and hunter in her own right. Their letters reveal an extraordinarily kind and generous couple fully devoted to exotic travel and lifelong learning. (Much more about the Lerners will be discussed in the following chapter.) The same year the Lerners made their way to Bimini for the first time, Kip Farrington, the very rich Louis Wasey, and charter boat captain Tommy Gifford visited, too, adding to the growing list of knowledgeable anglers who decided to see what the island had to offer. Rivkin writes that Farrington, Heilner, and Lerner "helped to pioneer the Bahamas fishery" and that "the first few years were a magical blend of tremendous fishing, manly camaraderie, and a great sense of adventure" (29). Word began to spread about the good times being had

Mike Lerner on June 20, 1935, with a blue marlin mount he donated to the American Museum of Natural History in New York.

over in Bimini, and the charter boat captains on the Florida coast took notice, especially after reports of the first big catches reached the Miami newspapers.

The First Pivotal Catches

The initial angling event that caught worldwide attention was Kip Farrington's February 28, 1933, catch of a 155-pound blue marlin, the first of the species to be successfully hooked, landed, and documented not just in Bimini but on the whole eastern side of the warm Gulf Stream (Watson 132). In *Fishing with Hemingway and Glassell*, Farrington classified the fish as "tiny" but "an eye-opener," as it established for the angling the world evidence that game fish could be caught in Bimini (3). Farrington's accomplishment was important because it garnered the attention of the other early sport-fishing figures, a small but intricately connected group of anglers. Just two weeks later, Betty Moore and Louis Wasey tag-teamed a 502-pound blue marlin, more than doubling the size of Farrington's fish (Saunders 163). These crucial events imprinted Bimini's name in the minds of the men and women who were in constant pursuit of their next great catch, and it did not take long for them to gas up their boats, set their compasses, and begin the trek to this new fishing mecca. Just like that, a new frontier in big-game fishing was christened.

The islanders were well aware of the infrastructure problem they faced if they wanted to comfortably accommodate an influx of anglers. They also recognized the flood of cash said anglers would represent for their economy, and their history as a community illustrates their willingness to adapt for the sake of survival. In 1922, the grand Bimini Bay Rod and Gun Club was completed, featuring 100 rooms and many attractive amenities. Sandra Davis writes the complex was "supposed to house the wealthy 'highball tourists' who would island hop the Bahamas by private yacht and seaplane to 'wet' party" among the "prohibition smugglers and gangsters who had the cash to spend" (Davis, "Bimini Rod and Gun Club Ruins"). The deadly 1926 hurricane pummeled the structure, however, and it was never reopened, mainly because business had not been brisk enough even before the disastrous storm. The construction of the resort was a decade too early to fully capitalize on the level of fishing tourism that was to come in the 1930s. Luckily for our story, the void was filled by Island Commissioner H. F. Duncombe and his wife Helen, who opened The Dower House in 1933, with Lerner registering as their first guest (Saunders, *Volume 1*, 121). Farrington included a glowing review of the property in his "Fishing at Bimini" chapter of *American Big Game Fishing*, saying it offered "splendid accommodations for anglers of both sexes" (127). Tragically, on November 18, 1934, The Dower House burned down. Not to be deterred, in 1935 the Duncombes opened The Compleat Angler, a legendary hotel of just 12

This picture of fishing boats at the Bimini dock in 1936 illustrates the atmosphere author John Dos Passos experienced the year before as he fished with Hemingway. Dos Passos wrote, "There were a few yachtsmen and sports fishermen about but the tiny island of Bimini proper was very much out of the world. There was a wharf and some native shacks under the coconut palms and a store that had some kind of a barroom attached, where we drank rum in the evenings" (62).

guest rooms that would become famous for illustrious guests such as Hemingway, who was known to book a room there to write in peace.

Another major obstacle facing the emergence of big-game fishing as a bona fide sport was the fact that the available gear (like fighting chairs and harnesses), tackle, and techniques had not evolved quickly enough to meet the demands of the kind of fishing these anglers wanted to do. The very deep waters of the Gulf Stream also made it possible for huge hooked fish to make runs into the depths, a phenomenon known as *sounding*. Those powerful maneuvers required the angler to fight that much harder to regain control. Bimini presented an especially problematic additional concern: its waters were absolutely overrun with sharks. Anglers who hooked into and fought record-breaking fish more often than not ended their battles shrouded in disappointment as the sharks tore into the tired game fish before they could be boated. The phenomenon of the ravenous sharks devouring all but the head and skeleton of the hooked fish came to be known as *apple coring*. As we will see in the next chapter, when Hemingway arrived in Bimini on the *Pilar* in 1935, he brought with him the technique, strategy, and sheer strength necessary to outwit the relentless sharks, and his innovation changed the Bimini fishing landscape forever. Once there, the fishing goals he established for himself were lofty. He wrote to Jane Mason on June 3, 1935, just after his arrival in Bimini, and proclaimed, "Still I would like to catch a thousand pounder" while acquiescing his goal might never be realized because "the sharks and the terribly deep water" were such impediments.

The island's inundation with eager fishermen ready to ply what were in those years maiden waters required more than just hotels and restaurants. Bimini needed to have numerous skilled and knowledgeable fishing guides available to accommodate the tourists who had no understanding of Bimini's underwater geography. Saunders explains, "The Bimini natives knew the waters but not the techniques of big game fishing, such as the twisting of wire, rigging of bait, boating a fish [and] the use of heavy tackle" (*Volume 1*, 163). Therefore, as charter boat captains began to figure out the optimal strategies and techniques, they trained local guides. From this early training grew a tradition of world-class fishing captains who have passed on their craft to future generations. To this day, Bimini's fishing guides are one of its greatest assets.

Hemingway with an apple-cored marlin caught by Mike Strater in mid-May 1935. This photo was taken on the beach at Cat Cay.

It is necessary to stop at this point and consider the historical situation of big-game fishing in the 1930s, a time when the world obviously was without the internet and social media. The only way for word to get out that Bimini had something so monumental to offer (beyond the letters, telephone calls, and personal conversations between the early anglers themselves) was through the books and magazine and newspaper articles that began to appear, first in a trickle and then in a flood. The big-game movement was gifted with extraordinary writers with the necessary fishing experience and the literary chops to convey their adventures in a compelling way. The first fundamental text with widespread impact was Zane Grey's 1927 *Tales of Swordfish and Tuna*. Even the title of the text reaches out and grabs the reader by the collar, tantalizing the audience with the promise of stories about hours-long clashes with gargantuan ocean beasts. Not surprisingly, Hemingway owned a copy (Reynolds 177). Born in 1872, Grey was the forerunning big-game angler and fishing writer. His death in 1939 was a great loss to the sport as he would have certainly continued to contribute his expertise. His ground-breaking experiences, including securing the honor of going down in history as the first man to capture a fish over 1,000 pounds with a rod and reel, and his trailblazing adventures in virgin waters (like fishing for particular species before other anglers ever thought to), situated him way ahead of his time in a multitude of ways ("Zane Grey"). For example, in 1926, he wrote a letter to Dr. William K. Gregory at the American Museum of Natural History announcing "Van Campen Heilner has finally persuaded me to donate my mounted fish to the Museum" (June 11, 1926, Central Archives, 1209, AMNH). This letter reveals Heilner and Grey were in contact with the best scientists in the world years before Hemingway began his association with the Academy of Natural Sciences and both he and Lerner began their work with the AMNH, collaborations that will be discussed fully later in this chapter.

Equivalently, Farrington's writing in the hands of fervent readers was a factor in Bimini's emergence as the promised land of fishing in the 1930s. He listed in *American Big Game Fishing* the kinds of fish one might catch in Bimini and when they were usually caught, teasing that "by the middle of May the lid blows off and you never know what size fish you may raise" (110). His chapter in this tremendously important book was without question the best free public relations release the island could have possibly received. Farrington declared, "It is practically a virgin field and this is only the third season it has been fished at all. When you stop to realize what the results have been up to this time [...], I venture to predict there will be more record fish taken out of these waters in the next ten years than any place else in the world" (110). He proclaimed the island was "the outstanding fishing center of the Atlantic Ocean" (110), a slogan Biminites would have been wise to print on T-shirts and commemorative mugs as soon as possible. It is important to remember as well that at this time, most people's conception of fishing involved catching a trout in a freshwater stream, hooking a catfish in a muddy lake, or reeling in a flounder at the coast. It did not occur to most that going out in a boat and hooking a 500-pound game fish and fighting it over the course of four or five hours was even a possibility. Imagine the excitement of discovering that your already beloved pastime could be taken to the next level in such a dramatic way on a dreamy island situated so close to the American mainland.

Hemingway Contributes to American Big Game Fishing

Notably, Hemingway contributed his own chapter to *American Big Game Fishing* titled "Marlin off Cuba." The influential volume was released on May 15, 1935. We pick up his story here even though he had not yet traveled to Bimini at the time when he composed the chapter. Hemingway first came to Key West in 1928 and had been living in his famous Whitehead Street home since 1931. At the time, his fishing expertise related only to freshwater angling, the kind he had grown up enjoying with his father. These Key West years delivered the formative saltwater fishing experiences Hemingway would need to participate in the sport with the level of acumen he desired. It is no secret that absolute mastery was his ultimate goal. He began by fishing from docks and the overseas bridges and then moved to offshore fishing in the boats of others (such as Josie Russell's *Anita*), as these were the days before he bought his beloved *Pilar*. Soon his interest expanded to the Cuban waters 90 miles to the south of the Conch Republic, and he began devoting sizable spans of time to learning to navigate and fish expertly. He began fishing for marlin in the waters north of Cuba in 1932. In Connett's volume, Hemingway claimed to have "first heard of the Cuban marlin fishing seven years ago" in the Dry Tortugas from Carlos Gutiérrez, whom he met on the trip (56). Because Hemingway's piece was likely written in 1934, this means he became aware of Cuban fishing immediately after arriving in Key West.

Hemingway did not just go over to Cuba to fish casually. Instead, he opted for an immersion experience, and as a result, he became one of the greatest anglers to ever fish those waters. The praise he received for his Cuban records came from the highest quarters. Heilner wrote that Hemingway "showed the world what marlin there were off the north coast of Cuba. The Cubans had known it for a long time, but they hadn't done much from a rod and reel standpoint" (131–32). The reader should take note of this idea of Hemingway bringing new knowledge to a fishing arena around a tiny tropical island because the same scenario will play out in Bimini later in our story. Farrington praised Hemingway's conquest of the Cuban fishing grounds, asserting the author "has fished these waters for many months with rod and reel, and has caught and seen more [marlin] than any one other sportsman. What is more important, he always makes it his business to find out all he can about them" (215). Hemingway's Cuban résumé

Hemingway poses with a marlin aboard Josie Russell's *Anita* in Key West in 1933. From left: Hemingway, Carlos Gutiérrez, Russell, and Joe Lowe.

stands as a testament to the expertise with which he fished. He already held the Cuban record for a 468-pound black marlin. As the decade progressed, Hemingway's approach to his angling education became very outward-looking toward a vision for big-game fishing as a whole. In William Braasch Watson's excellent "Hemingway in Bimini: An Introduction," he writes, "Until 1936 [. . .] Hemingway alone held the record, made off Havana, for the greatest number (seven) of white marlin ever taken in a day's fishing. Off Key West [in 1934] he landed the largest sailfish ever caught in the Atlantic (it weighed 119 ½ pounds), and off American Shoal, which is just north of Key West, he fought a world's-record mako shark [likely over 1,000 pounds] for five and a half hours before losing it" (134). Hemingway first fished in salt water in Key West in 1928, and by 1934, he secured an Atlantic record and had tangled with what would have been a world-record fish. By all accounts, his proficiency was achieved in a most accelerated fashion.

American Big Game Fishing is a fascinating time capsule that precisely illustrates the position of the emerging sport as it was on the cusp of exploding. By far, the best parts of Hemingway's chapter are the fishing charts he collaborated with famed wildlife artist and IGFA Hall of Famer Lynn Bogue Hunt to produce. In one illustration, Hemingway documented specific fishing locations and noted the ones that were worth a visit. Another set of pages reprinted Hemingway's personal photographs of mate Gutiérrez as he demonstrated how to properly prepare bait to troll for marlin. Hemingway's writing in the chapter is expert as well, and for the reader in 1935, his narrative would have evoked the feeling of a personal conversation with a great fisherman willing to share his most prized secrets. To ensure the reader had a hefty dose of reality, Hemingway reminded the audience about the time commitment great fishing requires — seasons rather than days. Though some years would yield great results and others would be a bust, he encouraged the reader to look on the bright side with him: "Happily, in fishing, there is always a season ahead" (67). Of all the wonderful nonfiction he composed, I argue Hemingway was at his best in this piece.

The well-deserved praise for Hemingway's contribution to the tome has been widespread. Contemporaneously, Farrington himself complimented Hemingway's piece within his own chapter in the book, calling the author's section "one of the greatest works ever written about [marlin]" and asserting no one "has had more experience or is better qualified to write about them" (116). Reiger's *Profiles in Saltwater Angling* continued the commendation of Hemingway's chapter in Connett's volume, saying, "The thoroughness of Hemingway's research, and the variety and interest of details couched in his lucid prose make this chapter one of the most satisfying monographs ever written on fish" (255).

This advancement in knowledge from 1928 to 1934 stands as one of the most remarkable characteristics of the Hemingway biography.

His aptitude as a dedicated student of the sport was attained during a time when a great deal was going on in his life, both professionally and personally: a son was born (Patrick, 1928), his father committed suicide (1928), *A Farewell to Arms* came out (1929), he broke his arm (1930), *The Fifth Column and the First Forty-Nine Stories* was published (1930), another son was born (Gregory, 1931), he settled in to a new house (1931), *Death in the Afternoon* was published *(1932)*, *Winner Take Nothing* was published (1933), and he spent 10 weeks on African safari (1933). Hemingway's brother Leicester explained that "no one was interested in big game fishing on the east coast [...]. Big game fishing needed someone with a lot of enthusiasm to promote it. Ernest Hemingway wanted to be that person" (Saunders *Volume 1*, 145). The author was willing to sacrifice a significant amount of his personal energy at an extraordinarily busy time in his life to be one of the leaders of the big-game fishing movement. The sport was fortunate to have such superb writers as Farrington, Heilner, Grey, and Hemingway as its mouthpieces during its infancy. While these crucial

Hemingway rests his right arm on the shoulder of mate Carlos Gutiérrez in Bimini.

early texts would have certainly enticed newcomers to the emerging sport and intrigued anglers who had never fished Bimini's waters before, the works had to also spur on those who had already experienced Bimini's splendor for themselves. I can say from firsthand experience that after trolling the Gulf Stream in January 2016, all I have been able to think about since then is my next Bimini adventure, and I only hooked several barracuda and a small tuna. Rereading these engaging writers during my research has ignited my imagination and a deep desire to return.

Essentially, Hemingway earned his big-game-fishing doctorate at a time when the field itself was still developing. He did not just want to learn how to catch the great fish — he wanted to know everything about them from a scientific standpoint. Because of his reputation and early writings about big-game fishing, it is remarkable that world-renowned scientists would not only hear of Hemingway but ultimately trust him to help facilitate their own scholarly work. His residency, so to speak, was completed as he served as a field research assistant for the Academy of Natural Sciences located in Philadelphia from 1934 to 1935. Lawrence H. Martin's fine article "Ernest Hemingway, Gulf Stream Marine Scientist: The 1934–35 Academy of Natural Sciences Correspondence" offers complete analysis of all Hemingway did to not only learn about marine science but to actually contribute to it. Martin explains that working in person and through letters with Charles M. B. Cadwalader, the Director of the ANS, and Henry W. Fowler, the ANS's chief ichthyologist, Hemingway contributed to the discovery of new species and the revision of official descriptions of these fish. Fowler even named a newly discovered species for Hemingway (*Neorithe hemingwayi*) to thank him for his help (Ott 48). Hemingway spent the whole month of August 1934 devoted to fishing with Fowler and Cadwalader out of Havana on the *Pilar*. According to Reynolds in *Hemingway in the 1930s*, this month of fishing was a learning experience for Hemingway because he was so used to having Josie Russell in control of the boat. Russell's considerable skill and his knowledge of "when and how to maneuver the boat to the angler's advantage" was taken out of the equation, and just four months after Hemingway took possession of his own boat, he was the captain of a scientific expedition (179).

Even other fishermen took notice of Hemingway's work with the museum. Hunt wrote in his "Sailfish" chapter for *American Big Game Fishing* of his hope that other anglers would be willing to collaborate with scientists in order to provide "the opportunity to study these fish as specimens fresh from the water, instead of being obliged to confine their researches to skins, mounted specimens, photographs, and too often, mere parts of the fish of which they are seeking knowledge" (13). Hemingway was serious about fishing, and the unwavering focus he devoted to marine research contributed to the conservation of species. While the word *conservation* may not have been in Hemingway's vocabulary, the scientists at the AMNH were already using the language in their letters, with the Vice-Director of the organization writing to a colleague about "conservation [. . .] as it relates to salt water fishing problems" in 1935 (W. M. Faunce to Orton G. Dale, Jr., February 11, 1935, Central Archives, 1267, AMNH). Hemingway's own research actually led to the ultimate "reclassification of marlin for the North Atlantic" (German). Furthermore, Nick Lyons writes in the introduction to *Hemingway on Fishing* that the author also "fished with Dr. Perry W. Gilbert, a shark expert and head of the Mote Laboratory in Sarasota, Florida" (*xxiii*). During this time, he "took careful notes on sharks and cataloged the principal kinds found in Cuban waters, their size range, and whether or not they were man-eaters, and if they would respond to shark repellents" (xxiv). The evidence outlined in the scholarship about Hemingway's scientific interest, his significant contributions to marine science, and his correspondence with esteemed scientists such as Cadwalader and Fowler handily dispel the myth of Hemingway as a shameless, selfish brute whose only concern was the next big fish he would get credit for boating.

The reader also sees from Hemingway's correspondence with Cadwalader and Fowler in 1934 the tremendous joy he reaped from his interdisciplinary hopscotching. He was obviously energized by his work in a completely different field from the arts and was invigorated by the opportunity to learn from and with such exceptional scientists. He wrote a September 6, 1934, letter to Cadwalader to make arrangements for specimen transfer and to request instructions for the proper preparation of the fish. Hemingway joked there was no need to rush because "Science is at least as long as Art" and reminded them accommodations could be made for the scientists to see the freshly caught fish in person. The precision with which Hemingway discussed the measurements, specimen, and various characteristics of the fish illustrates his commitment to his studies. The respect he gained for the museum staff is obvious as well. In the same letter to Cadwalader, he sang Fowler's praises and said he had never known "a better sportsman or a more agreeable companion" than Cadwalader. These were lofty words coming from a man like Hemingway who regarded the ideals of sportsmanship with such reverence.

Hemingway's devotion to the museum's research is also evident in his willingness to keep such detailed records with photographs of his catches. The technicalities and particulars referenced in these letters indicate he was focused wholeheartedly on analyzing the specimen. Hemingway suggested in an April 2, 1934, letter to Cadwalader, written while the author was on board the SS *Paris* en route back to America, that the notes he had been keeping for the Academy were "too extensive to put into a letter (and might bore you!)," but he would be willing to meet in New York later in the month for an in-person discussion. (We know from an April 9th Western Union cable to Cadwalader that the meeting did take place and from a July

9th letter to Fowler that he met with them in Philadelphia as well.) In the April 2nd note to Cadwalader, Hemingway asked the scientists to let him know "exactly what big game fish the museum holds" so he could begin his efforts to fill in the missing specimens. From the list, Hemingway would then attempt to catch and preserve the fish for study. He went to an incredible amount of trouble to save and then ship his unique catches to the museum. In an October 1, 1934, letter Hemingway wrote to Fowler from Cuba, he explained he had put a tuna on the ferry "to be re-iced in Key West" before it took the rest of the trip north to the museum. The reader can imagine that making arrangements in 1934 Cuba for a fish to be shipped to America would have been an onerous task. Hemingway pointed out additional hurdles to the process as well: fish spoil quickly in a tropical climate, the fisherman is "dead beat" when he comes in at night (the time when the work for the museum would need to begin), and the angler has to cut off valuable fishing time in the evening to return to the dock and still have enough light for accurate photographs and descriptions to be captured while the fish is fresh (Outgoing Correspondence, April 2, 1934, JFK). Hemingway asked for the museum to either send an academic proficient in skinning scientific specimen to do the job or to at least dispatch a person qualified to train Gutiérrez. The bulk of these letters demonstrate the terrific sacrifice Hemingway made to assist Cadwalader and Fowler and his willingness to work so hard for the simple reward of expanded personal and collective knowledge.

The best part of the museum letters for this reader is that even though Hemingway was corresponding with world-class scholars, he was still distinctly himself. In the September 6 letter to Cadwalader, he humorously described the excuses anglers make when they lose a fish, insisting that when such misfortune befell him, he would say the fish got away "in spite of all [. . .] science and skill could accomplish." He was not playing scientist, and he was not putting on false airs to attempt to compete academically; instead, he was just delighted to be part of what was a mutually beneficial partnership. Hemingway's service to the museum was invaluable, and Cadwalader and Fowler sharing their technical expertise undoubtedly made Hemingway an even more astute naturalist and fisherman.

A village scene of Bimini in 1937.

The letters Hemingway wrote and received in the early 1930s illustrate that he definitely knew what was going on in Bimini, and his interest was absolutely piqued. Reiger contends Hemingway first heard about Bimini in Key West from charter boat captain Bill Fagen and that Fagen's knowledge of the island came from fishing guide Charlie Thompson (11). Word about Bimini was definitely on the streets in Key West. Hemingway wrote to artist Mike Strater in July 1933 and referenced the fabulous fishing taking place in Bimini just on the other side of the Gulf Stream from where he was already fishing (Hendrickson 292). As a voracious magazine, newspaper, and book reader and a man consumed with learning as much as he could about big-game angling, Hemingway was reading authors such as Grey and Farrington who were writing about the happenings in Bimini. Beyond studying these outstanding authors, Hemingway was also beginning to correspond with them. In a letter Grey sent Hemingway on March 19, 1935, the reader can see the two had been talking about Bimini already. Grey encouraged Hemingway to go to Bimini and best his existing record so they could have the fun of competing. Some even suggest Grey dared Hemingway to join a global fishing challenge with him, an offer that was apparently refused but probably considered long and hard. This letter is an absolute gem, revealing a fascinating conversation between two of the top five fishermen in the world just two months before Hemingway made history in Bimini.

By the time he wrote his chapter for *American Big Game Fishing*, which would have likely been in 1934, Hemingway indicated an awareness of Bimini's growing fame by mentioning the experiences of Cuban greats Julio and Emilio Sanchez on the island (75). Reiger claims Hemingway was "still too preoccupied with Cuban marlin to pursue rumors of horse mackerel [giant bluefin tuna] in the Bahamas" (256). An interview with Leicester Hemingway conducted by Ashley Saunders confirms this fact. Hemingway's brother said the year was 1934, and Ernest said, "'I'm going to Bimini next spring. [...] But not until I get my hundredth fish. I'll probably fish here only another month if the weather stays good. Then I can write that piece.' The article he wanted to write was on marlin fishing for the *American Game Fishing* book [...]. He had already caught ninety marlin and wanted to have boated at least 100, so as to be writing from experience when that chapter was turned in" (*Volume 1*, 144). It is clear from this evidence that Hemingway wanted to be an aficionado before he ever set out for the Bahamas. We know from his writing in "Marlin off Cuba" that he succeeded in the goal he told his brother about, as he confirmed: "It was not until 1932 that we were able to put in a season after marlin in Cuba," but since that time he had "taken one hundred and one fish" (56–57). Bimini was hopping in the summer of 1934, and the stories coming out of the island (particularly about the elusive bluefin tuna that nobody could boat) were incredible. However, Hemingway did not go that summer even though he had the means to get there and the skill to fish as well as anyone else. He already owned a house about 150 nautical miles away from the destination. Chalk's Airlines could have flown him from Miami to Bimini in less than an hour. It appears as though he viewed Cuban waters as his training ground for the Super Bowl that awaited him in Bimini. He wanted to bring his best before he ever checked into the Bimini game — and he apparently wanted to be able to arrive on his own boat. The purchase of the *Pilar* in April 1934 changed everything for Hemingway. To even consider devoting a season to fishing at Bimini, he had to have his own boat. Watson suspects Hemingway "first wanted to try out his new boat in waters he already knew" in Cuba (133) before he attempted to tackle the unknown waters of

Hemingway and Carlos Gutiérrez at the wheel of the *Pilar* in 1934.

Bimini. His Cuban fishing aboard the *Pilar* in 1934 allowed him to become a proficient boatman. Lyons argues that access to a boat gave Hemingway "a much broader world, a much larger playing field with discrete challenges, a place to test brawn and courage and endurance" (xxiii). A strong argument can be made that Hemingway's confidence in his navigational and boating skills and in the capabilities of the *Pilar* was crucial to his overall success as a fisherman. While many others hired guides and chartered boats, Hemingway was competent enough on his own, and he had the luxury of fishing on the home turf of his own vessel.

That Hemingway did not just race over to Bimini right away says a great deal about his character and his devotion to the sport. The false parts of the Hemingway legend are built upon the image of an impulsive man who lacked self-control. It is too easy to latch on to the popular persona of Hemingway — the drinking, the womanizing, the trouble-making — and see a man without boundaries, discipline, or self-management. The true scholar of his work recognizes very quickly the tremendous control and discipline that guided so much of his life — the writing (obviously) and the remarkable amount of time he devoted to fully learning the sports and hobbies that enriched his life. There was nothing incidental about his sporting life. Instead, he actually approached it intellectually, and some would suggest religiously, though I choose not to go that far. In my view, there is much to learn from what I see as a very deliberate decision to pause at this juncture in his life.

We know 1935 was the year Hemingway finally loaded the *Pilar* with supplies and some of his closest friends and made the trip across from Key West to see Bimini with his own eyes for the first time. Kelly credits Erl Roman with finally talking Hemingway into making Bimini his destination in 1935 instead of Cuba, and that "after thanking [Roman] profusely, Hemingway seldom missed reading his *Miami Herald* columns" (59). McIver's outstanding *Hemingway's*

Key West claimed the trip was actually the alternate plan and that Hemingway had really intended to fish in Cuba that summer before political distress in the island nation changed his mind (119). In 1934 the presidency of Dr. Ramón Grau San Martín was usurped by Fulgencio Batista, a change that created an uncertain political climate Hemingway was wise to avoid. Hemingway's correspondence reveals 1934 was not a good year for fishing in general, and he may have decided to wait until conditions changed before he took his first Bimini trip. We also know the author wanted out of Key West for a little while. Hilary Hemingway and Carlene Brennen write in *Hemingway and Cuba* that around 1935, the author's fame was expanding. At the same time, "the tourists had discovered Key West and the city fathers had listed the Hemingway house on the visitors' map, and needless to say Papa was not pleased" (34). A change of scenery was definitely in order, and the natives of Bimini are certainly glad their island was the location Hemingway chose.

"I'll Be of Unsavoury Parentage. I'm Shot."

In order to prepare for his anticipated Bimini sojourn, Hemingway had outriggers installed on the *Pilar* in April 1935. Spreader outriggers (or beams projecting out from a boat to aid in fishing) were first developed by Tommy Gifford, and he was the first to catch an Atlantic blue marlin with them ("Thomas M. Gifford"). Shortly after the *Pilar* was readied, on April 7, 1935, Hemingway and his fishing party pointed her toward Bimini and left the Key West harbor behind. The IGFA library houses video footage of the crew's departure that day. What actually happened on that aborted attempt is perhaps my favorite Hemingway story because it provides the perfect stage on which his humanity and sense of humor are displayed. His unfortunate mishap brings to mind a saying we have in the South when an embarrassing event knocks someone down to size: "Well, I guess he puts his britches on one leg at a time just like the rest of us."

Captain Fred Lister, Ernest Hemingway, Carlos Gutiérrez, Captain Archie Cass, Mike Lerner, Captain Tommy Gifford, and Julio Sanchez stand in front of more than 1,500 pounds of blue marlin in Bimini in July 1935. This was the first time in history that four marlin of this size were photographed together.

On board were the great author John Dos Passos, Mike Strater, Albert "Bread" Pinder, and Richard Hamilton Adams. Some sources claim Katy Dos Passos was on the boat as well, but Brewster Chamberlin offers a convincing explanation to the contrary (157). The short version of the story is that a shark was hooked two hours out from Key West, and in Hemingway's attempt to shoot the animal with his .22-caliber Colt Woodsman, a terrible accident occurred. Apparently when the shark made a sudden jerk, Hemingway's shot missed the shark, "hitting instead a strip of metal along the boat's cockpit. The bullet broke into small pieces and ricocheted into Hemingway's legs" (McIver 120). The author's own account of the incident, published in *Esquire* in 1935 under the perfect title "On Being Shot Again," is absolutely hysterical and worth every second of the reader's time. In it, he reports his response after the injury was "I'll be of unsavoury parentage. I'm shot," though the reader does not need me to point out that his actual utterance was likely not nearly that sanitized. After offering advice on how to properly shoot horses, sharks, and other large beasts, Hemingway announced he had somehow managed to "[shoot] himself in the calves of both legs" (25). Luckily, he maintained a positive attitude long enough to write about the calamity for us. The humiliating incident forced the party to return to Key West and seek medical assistance for the wounds. The group again set out on April 15, 1935, this time with Charles Thompson replacing Strater and with Katy Dos Passos definitely on board.

The day the *Pilar* first docked in the crystal clear waters of Bimini after the journey from Key West was a historic day indeed. The great anglers already assembled there would have definitely known who Hemingway was and would have been aware of his presence. By the time Hemingway arrived on the island, Watson argues he was "no longer an apprentice in the sport but rather one of its leading practitioners, and his stay in Bimini that year did nothing to diminish his reputation" (133). What he found when he arrived was an island even more remote and undeveloped than Key West, which was attractive to a man in search of sport and seclusion. What followed that summer was the establishment of a sporting legacy so impressive that few anglers, if any, will ever surpass it.

FARRINGTON & COLEMAN

FORMERLY

SIMMONS & SLADE
ESTABLISHED 1895

SELWYN K. FARRINGTON
SHELDON T. COLEMAN
MEMBER N. Y. STOCK EXCHANGE
ALLEN B. KENDRICK
SELWYN K. FARRINGTON, JR.

52 BROADWAY

NEW YORK

TELEPHONE
WHITEHALL 4-2050

CABLE ADDRESS
"FARRCOLE"

June 20, 1935.

Mr. Erl Roman,
Care Maimi Herald,
Miami, Florida.

Dear Mr. Roman:

      I called you up when I arrived at Miami last Thursday night, but you had left for the day and I understood you had no telephone so was unable to get hold of you. I have wanted for a long time to have the pleasure of meeting the best fishing writer in the country and certainly look forward to that on my next trip.

      I am sorry if you did not get all of the details on the five tuna but I understood that the Giffords were trying to get the dope to you. We were in such an uproar all of the time, it was pretty difficult.

      I am enclosing you a picture of my Allison which weighed 96 pounds and took ten minutes on 36 thread, which I was very much pleased in catching never having believed I would ever be lucky enough to catch one.

      If you are in New York this summer be sure and look me up and come out with me for a day at Montauk and try for broad-bill. Will you please be good enough to send me one year's subscription to the Miami Herald starting with the June 1st, 1935 issue, forwarding same to above address.

      You might be interested in knowing that our fish taken were as follows:

S.K.Farrington, Jr. -	350	pounds,	48 minutes
"	400	" ,	1 hour, 51 minutes
"	542	" ,	3 hrs, 40 minutes
Philip Holden	420	" ,	65 minutes
Louis Ripley	460	" ,	75 minutes

All of these fish were taken on the same Ashaway Line, 3000 feet of 54 thread and 16-0 Edward VomHofe reels, which worked magnificently. Two of them were taken on the Hardy 24 oz. bamboo and the three others on the 28 oz. Edward Vom Hofe hickory which is by far the better rod.

This lovely letter was sent from Kip Farrington to Erl Roman on June 20, 1935. In it Farrington classifies Hemingway as having "no equal as a fisherman or sportsman."

In how many bodies of water could you see three of the
four great game fish of the world on three successive days?
Only one other place to my knowledge, New Zealand;
[. . .] Travel over 7,000 miles if you care to, but leave me
at Bimini on the way.

— Kip Farrington, *American Big Game Fishing*

III
Hemingway's Three Bimini Summers:
Big-Game Fishing's "Camelot"

AS A PROFICIENT practitioner of big-game fishing when
he made that first Bimini trip in the spring of 1935, Hemingway was cognizant of the major obstacle he would have
to mediate: sharks. The problem was two-fold. First, sharks prefer the
waters around Bimini for the same reasons game fish like to hang out
there: water clarity, warmth, and food supply. *Shark-infested* was an
adequate appraisal of the Bimini situation in the 1930s, and sharks
were the top concern of anglers there. Secondly, the available tackle
at the time was inadequate to meet the demands of Bimini fishing.
Farrington wrote of the great tuna the anglers sought, "none of these
magnificent fish have ever been boated near Bimini unmarked by
sharks and most of those hooked have made their get away on account
of [tackle] being bitten in two by other fish in the school" ("Fishing
at Bimini" 111). Day revealed in "Bimini, Bahamas: Hemingway's
Island in the Stream" that "equipment was primitive, tackle was inadequate, and [most] boats [. . .] lacked both outriggers and a flybridge.
There was no big game reel. The tuna door was unknown" (7). The

greatest minds were needed to figure out the appropriate tackle setup for Bimini's particular angling stage. The window to catch the really big tuna was minute, with their migration through Bimini toward cooler water starting in May and running through June. Hemingway was determined to make the most of their run, employing the philosophy that working "close to the breaking point of your tackle" without breaking it separated the great anglers from the rest of the pack ("Fishing at Bimini" 67). Fundamentally, the predicament was that fishermen were having to fight for too long to get their catches to the boat because of the inferior gear. When fish were first hooked, they were strong and fast enough to elude predators, sometimes for incredibly long periods of time. After hours of fighting, though, the exhausted fish represented a very easy meal for the frenzy of waiting sharks. What Hemingway brought to the equation in that legendary summer of 1935 was the solution for the Bimini shark predicament: a technique that would counteract the sharks and the limitations of the tackle.

In *Papa: A Personal Memoir*, Hemingway's son Gregory relayed advice Mike Lerner had offered his father: "Ernest, you have to bring these fish up fast. After they're hooked they make one long sounding run, go almost straight down, and die down there from the pressure of the depth. Then you have to bring up anywhere from four to eight hundred pounds of dead weight [...] — and you have to do it before the sharks get the blood scent. [...] No one has ever landed an unmutilated tuna here" (27). This sage advice came from Lerner in Hemingway's first month in Bimini during the summer of 1935. Hemingway's physical stature and strength and his iron-clad will to succeed helped him to execute Lerner's prescription to "bring these fish up fast." Quite simply, Hemingway's strategy was to do everything possible to bring in the fish at lightning speed, no matter what physical abuse the angler had to endure in the process. Once his no-holds-barred approach was proven successful, the fish caught using the notorious technique were said in the fisherman's vernacular to be "Hemingwayed." Farrington's insight about Hemingway's method is particularly useful here because he was on the island with the author that summer pursuing the same goal:

> He had the strength and he really could handle his fish, and he was a great boy for trying to keep thirty seconds or a minute ahead of them and out-think them. I learned this lesson from him: if you can think what they are going to do a little bit ahead of when they do it, it is most advantageous. He also gave me the idea that for every minute the angler laid off the pressure or eased off the drag for a rest, it was as good as a five-minute respite for the fish. (*Fishing with Hemingway and Glassell* 6–7)

Because of his proactive thinking, Hemingway created a scenario in which the hooked fish could manage to stay ahead of the sharks while the angler had time to reel it in more quickly. The reader can gain a frame of reference for the physical toll this kind of fishing took on the body in Farrington's chapter in *American Big Game Fishing*. He provided advice for the angler who was considering going to Bimini, recommendations that included hitting the gym in the weeks before for strength training and soaking his or her hands in brine twice a day for a few weeks before the trip ("Fishing at Bimini" 125). Context is again important here because these anglers were not going on a day-long fishing trip of a few hours like so many short-term vacation charters. They devoted whole seasons to their pursuits, their days beginning before sunrise and concluding after sunset. These days were often filled with hours-long battles with monstrous fish under the blistering tropical sun. These were not pleasure cruises but voyages for intensely demanding and rugged sport. Apparently, Hemingway had some fitness work to do before he went to Bimini as well. Carlos

Baker described a January 1935 trip through New Orleans in which the author put on quite a few pounds enjoying more than his share of "The Big Easy's" food and drink, a binge that was no doubt well worth it but which required him to "[get] back into shape" afterwards (346). In my view, there is no shame in any pound gained in a gourmand city.

Hemingway's approach also included considering factors beyond the performance and technique of the angler and the tackle he or she was using. He began to think critically about the role of the boat. He had a theory that a secondary vessel could be used in tandem with the main boat once an extra-large game fish was hooked. The angler could transfer to a fighting chair in the smaller craft, hold on, and let the fish pull him like an Alaskan sled dog. The fish, he reasoned, would tucker out by pulling so much weight through the water. He even towed a skiff to Bimini with him behind the *Pilar* with the intention of attempting the maneuver, though there is no evidence he ever executed the plan (Hendrickson 308). John Patrick Hemingway says Ernest Hemingway "was one of the first to use the technique of putting the boat into full reverse to get his catch out of the water as soon as possible." Hemingway and Farrington developed the first strategies for managing the boat in relationship to the fish to minimize its vulnerability to sharks (Rivkin 24). A wonderful letter from Lerner to Hemingway in December 1935 includes hand-drawn sketches that outline his theories about the most advantageous boat positions for the captain to maintain while assisting the angler. It was imperative for the successful fishing outfit to include an adept crew, which is why Hemingway was so dedicated to the mates he came to trust. A skilled angler's best hours-long effort could be thwarted in seconds by a crew member who did not perform his job competently. These early anglers methodically dissected every element of their performance in the quest to improve their strategy.

Just three weeks after Hemingway arrived in Bimini, a month after being shot in both legs and a few weeks before he proved to the world his technique would be successful, he had an opportunity to fight what would have been a world-record tuna likely weighing more than 1,000 pounds. The best extended narrative about the event can be found in Chapter 7 of Hilary Hemingway and Carlene Brennen's gorgeous book *Hemingway in Cuba*. The kernel of the story is that late one evening, Hemingway came upon Charlie Cook, the manager of Cat Cay, a private luxury development about 10 miles south of Bimini. Cook had been fighting the fish for more than six hours and was ready to yield to the animal and give up when Hemingway volunteered to take over the rod, reportedly telling Cook he wanted the chance to fight the fish "not for the record, but to learn from him" (46). The story ended in heartbreak and anger, with Hemingway

Hemingway, Pauline, and all three boys pose with four blue marlin caught by three different anglers on July 20, 1935. The picture was taken on Brown's dock, and only the left two fish — the smaller of the four weighing in at 362 pounds and 330 pounds, respectively — were caught by Hemingway (Hendrickson 283). Mike Lerner and Julio Sanchez caught the other two.

The first unmutilated tuna caught in Bimini on May 21, 1935
(not 1934 as the handwritten note suggests).

being able to bring the fish close enough to the boat to see it just as the sharks began to circle. Despite a hail of gunfire aimed at scaring the hungry scavengers away, they took all of the tuna except the head, which alone weighed 249 pounds (50). The experience was a formative one, giving the author the chance to battle what would have been a record-holder and to face off with Bimini's relentless sharks.

As big-game anglers struggled to get their footing on the Bimini fishing grounds, the question of mutilation and how it should impact record catches was considered in print articles and in the correspondence between fishermen. In the June 1936 issue of *Outdoor Life*, Hemingway himself wrote about the issue of mutilation as it relates to world-record fish. In the piece, he advocated for three classes of record fish: one for the base size and weight for the fish taken in any way, the second for the size and weight of the fish caught on a rod and reel with assistance from an outside party, and the third for the size and weight of the fish taken on rod and reel without assistance from an outside party (70). In the case of mutilation after the fish has been brought to the edge of the boat, the author was still of the opinion that the angler should get credit for the record, with the penalty for the intervention being the weight the fish lost in the attack. He was not, however, of a mind to credit an angler for a fish the sharks killed (71). He contended that he took no side in the debate because he fished "for fun, not for records" while expressing his wish for fishermen to just stop bickering and decide on acceptable standards (71–72). That Hemingway was thinking so much about world records was the result of the formation and activities of the early fishing clubs, the development of which will be plotted in the next chapter.

The First Unmutilated Tuna

Everything Hemingway wrote — whether it was his personal letters, his boat log, magazine articles, book chapters, prefaces and forewords, or his fiction — illustrated that he was consumed by lifelong learning, and he no doubt was soaking up every ounce of knowledge he could from those first weeks in Bimini as he faced new obstacles and recovered from his bullet wounds. May 21, 1935 turned out to be the culmination of his investment as he set the world on fire with an incredible feat: catching the first unmutilated tuna to ever be boated in Bimini. Farrington predicted in 1935 that the great tuna would be captured whole and very soon. "I firmly believe," he wrote, "that these fish will be taken unscarred in Bimini waters [...] and the spring of 1935 will only be the beginning" ("Fishing at Bimini" 112). Hemingway's catch was a 381-pound bluefin tuna. His excitement can be seen in his 11-word telegram the next day to Baron Bror von Blixen as he announced a boating time of 70 minutes (Hemingway to von Blixen, May 22, 1935, JFK). Farrington called Hemingway's accomplishment "one of the outstanding feats in the annals of Atlantic Coast fishing" (*Atlantic Game Fishing* 191). Kelly writes in *Florida's Fishing Legends and Pioneers* the "ensuing publicity circled the globe until everyone involved in the big-game fishing circles knew about it" (59). Just two days later, Hemingway bagged another unmutilated bluefin, this one weighing 319 pounds. In a letter to Jane Mason from Key West on June 3, 1935, he informed her that the fish was boated in just over 45 minutes. (The reported weights of these fish vary wildly among different sources. I have opted to use evidence from Hemingway's letters and his account of these catches in his article about the events (including pictures) from the August 1935 edition of *Esquire* ["*He Who Gets Slap Happy*"].) Farrington claimed he then followed Hemingway with three more catches weighing 330, 400, and 542 pounds, the final unmutilated tuna caught in Bimini during the 1935 season (*Fishing with Hemingway and Glassell* 4–5). Hemingway affirmed Farrington's assertion in the same *Esquire* piece but listed the size of Farrington's last fish as 545 pounds (182).

These historic catches for Hemingway and Farrington during the "Summer of the Tuna" put the eyes of the fishing world firmly on them as the pace-setters to beat and sounded the official alarm about Bimini for the fishing fraternity. Heilner explained, "Everyone believed it was impossible to land a whole tuna on account of the sharks and then the next year Ernest Hemingway and Kip Farrington put the Indian sign on them" (158). Ashley Saunders explained to me "bringing in [these tuna] unmutilated really opened up the eyes of a lot of fishermen and caused them to come to Bimini." Gregory Hemingway says of the festive scene at the dock when his father brought in the first unmutilated tuna that the crowd praised the author's triumph, and "Mike [Lerner] not only thought that it was an extraordinary feat but that it would do a lot for Bimini, now that fishermen knew that tuna could be brought up unmutilated" (29). The author himself was rightfully elated with his success, announcing in *Esquire* "the Great Myth that you cannot catch [tuna] in a half mile or a mile of deep water is dispelled" ("He Who Gets Slap Happy" 182). That Bimini summer also saw Hemingway bring in a 786-pound mako shark, the second largest ever landed anywhere and a North American record for the species. The amazing catch, which was only 12 pounds short of the world record, took place on June 22, 1935, just a month after he brought in the first unmutilated tuna.

The Hemingway-Lerner Friendship Begins

The second most important event of the 1935 summer, beyond the unmutilated tuna breakthrough, was Hemingway's initial meeting with Mike Lerner. Rivkin reports Mike and Helen Lerner had first started fishing for big game in the early 1930s, and after "hearing stories about giant tuna and marlin traveling virtually unmolested along the Bimini shoreline, their subsequent visit to that tropical paradise [changed] their lives" (36). According to Hilary Hemingway and Carlene Brennen, the author met Lerner immediately after coming ashore in Bimini for the first time (42). The seeds of friendship sown that day bloomed in the following decade in remarkable ways.

At the time Hemingway and Lerner met in the spring of 1935, the famous Lerner Anchorage — the fishing compound constructed on the King's Highway — was not yet complete. Many scholars suggest the Lerners initially owned a house on Cat Cay before their home on North Bimini was commissioned and that Hemingway lodged there with them. However, this arrangement would have been unworkable for a number of reasons. Cat Cay was first visited by Lou Wasey in 1931, and a few years later when it opened as an invitation-only island, it was according to Peter Benchley "the WASP dream — the most chic, most exclusive, most expensive private resort in the Western Hemisphere" (26). It was so exclusive, in fact, that the dockmaster was instructed to ask incoming vessels if there were

Hemingway is photographed with a 786-pound mako shark caught at Bimini in June of 1935. The comparison of the size of the rod, the stature of the man, and the enormity of the shark — one of the strongest creatures on earth — allows the viewer to understand the fight involved in these historic battles. Two hundred pounds of man would challenge 700 pounds of mako shark with only a primitive rod in between them.

any Jewish people aboard. If so, the boat would not be allowed to come into port (26). Sadly, it would have been impossible for Michael Lerner, as a Jew, to even visit Cat Cay, much less own a home there. Some historians also erroneously assert the Anchorage was completed in 1933, the same year the Lerners first visited the island. If they could have purchased land, drawn up plans for a home, and had it constructed in less than a year's time (which seems nearly impossible), Mike Lerner would not have needed to be Helen Duncombe's first guest at The Dower House, as we know he was. The correspondence between Lerner and Hemingway also proves the Anchorage was not finished at least by late August 1935, the last time the author was in Bimini that year. Hemingway wrote to Lerner on May 19, 1936, about his imminent Bimini trip and expressed that he was "crazy to see [the] new house." While these historical facts and dates might not seem to be very consequential, they are vital to constructing a Hemingway timeline in Bimini supported by accurate evidence.

If there is any one structure that could be designated as the most important in the development of big-game fishing as a worldwide sport, the Anchorage wins hands down. Hemingway and Brennen aptly characterize it as "the unofficial embassy of the island" (42). The Lerners turned it into a fishing retreat and invited the very best anglers in the world to convene there, stay for free, enjoy the food and drink, and participate in what had to be the most interesting conversations. As I stood on the porch of the Anchorage looking out over the Gulf Stream, it was not difficult to imagine the late-night storytelling, the wild laughter in the humid tropical night, and the ice-cold cocktails that were certainly flowing. The world's most skilled anglers were often in residence at the Anchorage, including Kip Farrington, Erl Roman, Tommy Shevlin, Julio Sanchez, and Lynn Bogue Hunt (Rivkin 37 and 44–45). Add Mike and Helen Lerner and Ernest Hemingway to the mix, and the result had to be pure magic. Hemingway even managed to lure the lovely Jane Mason to Bimini with letters highlighting its splendor. Interestingly, it was in Bimini (at The Compleat Angler bar) that Mason was introduced by Pauline Hemingway to Arnold Gingrich, who eventually became Mason's fourth husband.

The Anchorage in 1936 before the paving of the King's Highway.

While Hemingway was on the island during the summers of 1935–37, he had other housing options aside from bunking on the *Pilar* (even while hosting multiple guests like the von Blixens and Strater in that first summer) or staying in one of the houses on the Lerner property once construction was finalized). He was known to book his favorite room at Helen Duncombe's The Compleat Angler hotel, but that reservation was made mainly to secure a quiet writing space, especially when Pauline and his boys were on the island, or to evade bad weather when he slept on the *Pilar*. Gregory Hemingway asserted that once he and his brothers arrived, the boat was kept at The Compleat Angler's dock (25). Ansil Saunders reveals Helen Duncombe "didn't particularly like Hemingway" because he was too rough for her, and she was aware of his propensity to start fistfights. Ansil says that because her establishment catered to the very rich, having Hemingway causing trouble was bad for business. The author also had the option of staying out on Cat Cay. He spent time there with his family because he had contacts with several of the wealthy home owners in the private resort. Aside from its pristine beauty and considerable level of seclusion, Cat Cay is also on "Tuna Fish Alley," the fabled waters that were once known as the best place on the planet to catch bluefin tuna. The Hemingway boys also liked to stay at the "Blue Marlin Cottage," an adorable little bungalow that is part of the Anchorage complex. Finally, some islanders also reference a smaller cottage on the Lerner property near Brown's dock where Hemingway sometimes bunked.

Trying to piece together exactly where Hemingway stayed, with whom, and for how long while he was in Bimini is an impossible task. When he first arrived on the island, we know from his letters that he slept on the *Pilar* and retreated to The Compleat Angler as necessary. Letters to friends such as Jane Mason, Henry Fowler, and Arnold Gingrich in 1935 indicate he spent his time in Bimini as opposed to Cat Cay, often sleeping on the *Pilar*. In the summer of 1936, he split his time between Bimini (at the Anchorage), Cat Cay, and sleeping

Pauline and Gregory Hemingway exit a Chalk's seaplane in the Bimini Harbor.

on the boat with Gutiérrez. Similarly, evidence suggests he lodged in Bimini and Cat Cay in 1937. We know, too, that he resided with the Lerners at the Anchorage in the summer of 1937.

The Lerner-Hemingway relationship will be examined closely in the next three chapters, but it is necessary to discuss here how much influence the two had on each other, an impact that would eventually extend to the entire big-game community when the International Game Fish Association was born. Once Lerner and Hemingway joined forces in Bimini, they were an unstoppable fishing duo. In *Saltwater Gamefishing Offshore and Onshore,* Peter Goadby portrays the pair as "masters of angler aggression, fighting with maximum drag [and] dominating the fish techniques on heavy tackle" (121). When they were not fishing together in Bimini, they wrote each other pages-long letters outlining their latest theories, strategies, and tackle preferences as they tried to figure out how to land even bigger fish. Lerner wrote to Hemingway on December 4, 1935, hypothesizing

A photograph of the Anchorage in 1937, taken from the Queen's Road vantage point looking up the hill toward the open ocean.

about the number of Bimini anglers snapping their line because of their use of drag and the effects of friction due to the speed of the fighting fish. This letter was penned six months after Hemingway brought in the first unmutilated Bimini tuna, yet that feat did not satisfy all of the questions anglers had about the island's unique fishing challenges. For Hemingway and Lerner, these momentous catches inspired them to push harder and innovate further. Hemingway seemed in these years to be consumed by the intellectual obstacles he was forced to negotiate. He wrote in "The President Vanquishes" for *Esquire* of his supposition that big fish were being lost by great anglers in Bimini because they were using leaders that were too long (167). While his private conversations in letters with friends like Lerner were sorting through every eventuality and innovation, his public writing in forums such as *Esquire* continued the larger dialogue about improving best practices within the sport for everyone.

Hemingway's tuna catch did not mean the angler's struggles with the Bimini sharks were over. Hemingway and Lerner's goals moved into the 1,000- and 1,100-pound range, and their letters almost constantly encouraged each other to catch bigger fish. Hemingway informed Lerner in a March 23, 1936, letter that he had recently seen the businessman in the newspaper next to a game fish "that didn't look quite big enough." To remedy the situation in the future, the author suggested Lerner should just recycle some of the bigger fish he had previously captured for the photographs because he did not "look right [. . .] with anything under four hundred pounds." Even as they ribbed each other, they continued to think critically about how to land record-breaking fish with the same challenging tackle in the face of the sharks. Lerner even speculated in the December 4th letter that the *granders* may never be boated in Bimini because of the sharks and the tremendous depth of the water. One of the great pleasures of reading their correspondence is observing how they put their heads together in an attempt to solve such complex problems, and they were perhaps the two best people on the planet at that time to be having those discussions.

What brought them together was more than just a love for fishing. They both had a fervent desire to see the sport of big-game fishing become more organized, with a code of conduct for ethical angling and a vetted and trustworthy process for certifying and maintaining world records. This shared desire ultimately was the genesis of the IGFA. Hemingway's interest in expanding what was known about marine science was an area of enthusiasm that Lerner also shared. The first summer Hemingway was on the island is the same year that Lerner began his association with the American Museum of Natu-

Pauline Hemingway cuts her husband's hair at the Anchorage in 1937.
This photograph was taken at the end of their marriage.

ral History in New York. Rivkin describes Lerner's realization that marine science was in need of advancement and characterizes him as "startled by the woeful lack of research facilities dedicated to marine studies" (40). Lerner began working with the Museum on several expeditions — seven in all — that taught scientists a great deal about big-game species, and both he and Helen went along and served as an integral part of the research team. Like Hemingway's previous collaboration with the Academy of Natural Sciences in Philadelphia, Lerner's AMNH partnership (which would eventually include Hemingway, who worked with the museum at least until 1943) represented a time of tremendous growth in knowledge about species. These expeditions provided multifaceted data about never-before-studied behaviors of large saltwater fish. The relationships formed as the work was completed and the success of the collaboration ultimately led to the foundation of the superb Lerner Marine Laboratory in Bimini.

The Lerner Marine Laboratory

Though the physical structure of the Lerner Marine Laboratory was not completed until 1948, Lerner's idea for it had been percolating many years before. The first evidence I was able to locate in the correspondence mentioning a lab is a letter from Lerner to Hemingway on April 2, 1937, from Cape Town, South Africa. At the invitation of Lerner, Francesca LaMonte, a trailblazer who at the time was one of only five women working as ichthyologists, came to Bimini in July with two other AMNH scientists to focus their research on marlin. Lerner promised to erect some sort of structure they could use on the island. The Lerners made arrangements at the Anchorage (both in their home and in external tents) to accommodate the scientific work. In a 1937 report to the AMNH director housed at the American Museum of Natural History Library, LaMonte outlined the events of the trip, explaining the Lerners had "cleared out the tackle room of their own guest house, and had re-arranged it as an indoor laboratory for us," as well as offering "good table and shelf space, storage space for our cans and heavy equipment, and the use of a lavatory and shower" (LaMonte 1). She also mentioned a tent with mosquito protection that was erected outside. The report indicated Helen and Michael Lerner caught most of the 24 blue marlin the group was able to study (2). The Lerners' generosity was displayed in their willingness to have "a glass-bottomed skiff constructed for" the scientists when

The Lerner Marine Laboratory

it became clear they could not dive safely with the equipment they brought, considering the predatory fish in the water (3). This report provides a wonderful illustration of the expedition and demonstrates just how important collaborations with big-game anglers were to the AMNH scientists. These temporary accommodations could be interpreted as Michael Lerner's initial move toward a facility on the island for the scientific study he realized was so important.

Once finished in 1948, the Lerner Marine Laboratory was a world-class facility, which was due in large part to the Lerners' financial generosity toward the project. It is said one of Mike Lerner's goals was to use the lab's research to investigate a possible cure for cancer, which afflicted his brother. The facility of 1948 included the laboratory and apartments for resident scientists. In later years, new buildings were constructed to add "storage sheds, machine and carpenter shops, cottages for the resident director and engineer, laundry facilities and a library" (Saunders *Volume 1,* 135). The scientific agenda of the lab and the facilities used to complete its work — including "a darkroom, dissecting facilities, a specimen pool with more than 1,500 living examples of marine life open to public view, and one of the first closed-circuit TV connections" for visitors to watch fish swimming

The dedication ceremony of the Lerner Marine Laboratory took place on March 29, 1948. Lerner later turned over the lab to the American Museum of Natural History along with a considerable endowment.

underwater — were cutting-edge (Rivkin 55). In 1963, the lab was able to purchase a 65-foot research boat called the *J. A. Oliver* to conduct extended research offshore, and in 1969 a 100-foot pier with shark pens was also added (Rusk 24). For the 21st-century reader, these amenities might not seem so impressive, but at the time, the Lerner Marine Laboratory was unusually advanced and groundbreaking.

The lab employed local Biminites in various ways, including as assistants to gather live specimens for study (Wylie, *The Lerner Marine Laboratory* 15). Thomas Saunders, a lifelong resident of the island, worked as a handyman and painter for the Lerners for many years and was an employee at the lab for four years. He told me the facility "had doctors from around the world, and because it was there so long, they wanted to put something back into the island, so they had evening classes for us [the locals] for five years. It would last from 5 in the evening until 11 at night. That was an extension for education, because actually, the way we are set up here, you go to school until grade six, never any college or high school. So we were lucky to get that extra education." Saunders learned how to train dolphins at the lab, and he points out they had the "first captive dolphins in the Bahamas. Bimini here was 60 years ahead of Atlantis," the well-known Bahamian mega-resort that offers tourists swimming experiences with dolphins. Saunders trained two dolphins in particular for the U.S. Navy, teaching them how to take a rescue donut out to a boat. Throughout his adult life, Lerner did a great deal to support the Armed Forces, including working with the military to design fishing kits both for emergency situations and for the enjoyment of deployed soldiers.

The Lerner Marine Laboratory closed unexpectedly in the 1970s, likely the victim of governmental budget politics. (Sources conflict about the exact closing date, which was sometime between 1972 and 1975.) As with all field stations, the outcomes of the research are constantly weighed against the costs they require, and the

Kip Farrington (far right) posed in a promotional photograph for the emergency fishing survival kit the IGFA helped develop for the U.S. Navy. In case of a castaway situation, the kits would provide the soldier with means to fish for food.

work being done in Bimini was expensive. The closing of the facility had to pain Mike Lerner, who devoted the best years of his life to the island of Bimini and to the work of the laboratory. He passed away from cancer in Miami on April 16, 1978, at the age of 87, having lived an extraordinary life. His genius, generosity, and perseverance improved the lives of many not only during his lifetime but for generations to come.

If you would like to learn more about the fascinating scientific work conducted in Bimini, you should read Philip Wylie's 1960 informational booklet about the facility called *The Lerner Marine Laboratory at Bimini Bahamas*. Included are intriguing photographs of the researchers conducting experiments, examining fish in the live wells, and working in the field. As a Bimini Heritage plaque in front of the former laboratory building reminds the present-day visitor, the results of these efforts led to many important discoveries that still have an impact on marine studies today.

Mike Lerner works with a dolphin at the Lerner Marine Laboratory.

The "Big Fat Slob" of Bimini

With a personality like Hemingway spending parts of three summers on the island, it was inevitable that the stories about his time there would grow to almost mythical proportions. It is hard to believe, but history proves many of these legends are grounded pretty firmly in the truth. Plenty of evidence documents the struggles Hemingway faced in later years with his declining mental and physical health; the Bimini stories, however, are a happy reminder that he was able to string together many very contented years experiencing life completely on his own terms.

The greatest of the Hemingway legends in Bimini involves a very famous fistfight that took place on May 26, 1935, on the Government Dock in Alice Town between Hemingway and Joseph Knapp, the publisher of a number of important American magazines like *Collier's* and *McCall's*. Thankfully, the main witness to the event was songwriter and calypso singer Nathaniel Saunders, affectionately known on the island as "Piccolo Pete" or "Uncle Natty." Despite Paul Hendrickson's report in his 2011 book *Hemingway's Boat* that Natty Saunders "has passed" (311), I am pleased to report he is still alive at the time of this writing (though his health and mobility have declined significantly). It was one of the great honors of my life to interview him in early 2016 and spend a little bit of time with him. He was born on November 7, 1914, so at the time of our interview at his home on the Queen's Highway, he was 101 years old. A Bahamian newspaper article announcing his 100th birthday in 2014 described him as "the community['s] oldest, most respected and entertaining personality" and "the backbone of the Bimini community" ("100 Year Old Nathaniel 'Piccolo Pete' Saunders"). When you ask anyone on the island about Nathaniel Saunders, he is described with absolute reverence.

Though his voice is weak and his mind drifts in and out of clarity, hearing him call up those distant memories was a magnificent experience. All I had to do was ask him to tell me about Hemingway. "We called him Papa Hemingway — Papa," he began. His recollection immediately took him to that infamous day on the Bimini dock: "Mr. Knapp called Hemingway a 'big fat slob,' and Hemingway balled his fists." He went on to describe Hemingway as "a man who liked to see activity. He liked boxing." From there, he broke into a rendition of his uproarious song, "Big Fat Slob," and at the conclusion, was pleased to announce, "I wrote that song." The lyrics chronicle the scuffle that took place between Hemingway and Knapp. By all accounts, Knapp was thoroughly inebriated, and Hemingway did what he could to diffuse a physical fight (at least for a time). Natty Saunders suggests the rub between Hemingway and Knapp was due to the fact that they had both entered the harbor that day with potential record-holders — Hemingway's a wahoo and Knapp's a white marlin (Saunders *Volume 2*, 74). It appears Knapp's drunken state turned what should have been a friendly conversation about two great catches into a series of sour exchanges. Knapp's heckling became too much to bear, and Hemingway silenced it with a series of punches that knocked Knapp out cold. By the time evening fell and Piccolo Pete and the Sugarfoots were singing their latest hit, the event transitioned from a dockside scuffle into a full-blown island hootenanny. In those days, it was tradition for talented locals to improvise songs on the dock to con-

"Uncle Natty" Saunders was happy to talk to me at his Bimini home in January 2016. He was 101 years old at the time of our interview.

gratulate anglers for their prize fish (Doty, "Part Three," 53). When the fight (which mostly involved Hemingway hitting and Knapp enduring the punches before blacking out) took place, Hemingway had been on the island just a little bit over a month. Even today, word of an unusual visitor spreads quickly on the island. The Biminites who did not know about Hemingway at sunup on May 26, 1935, certainly did by sundown. Saunders's "Big Fat Slob" recording (the lyrics of which are included below) is available on iTunes and Spotify on his excellent album called "Bimini Nights," and you should buy it now and save it for a day when you really need to smile.

Natty Saunders refused to let us leave his home without a gift. We were sent away with this treasure, an autographed political banner.

Bimini Boxing

Hemingway is also credited with introducing boxing to the islanders, and the tales about the matches he organized are among the favorites of the residents. In a personal interview with Ashley Saunders, he explained the author "brought boxing gloves here in 1936 and taught

---

"Big Fat Slob"

Mr. Knapp called Mr. Ernest Hemingway
A big fat slob
Mr. Ernest Hemingway balled his fist
And gave him a knob
Big fat slob in Bimini
This the night we have fun

Oh the big fat slob in Bimini
This the night we got fun

Mr. Knapp look at him and try to mock
And from the blow
Mr. Knapp couldn't talk
At first Mr. Knapp thought
He had his bills in stalk
And when Mr. Ernest Hemingway walk
The dock rocked
Mr. Knapp couldn't laugh
Mr. Ernest Hemingway grin
Put him to sleep
With a knob on his chin

Lyrics and tune written by Nathaniel Saunders

the natives how to box. These things are what the people admire him for." The folk tales vary on the amount wagered, with some saying $200, $250, or $300, but Saunders confirms that

> Hemingway put up a standing offer of a hundred-dollar bill for any native that could go three rounds with him. And nobody [won], and he knocked out two of my uncles. He knocked out Willard Saunders, who was one of the strongest men in Bimini. And he knocked out John Duncombe. Both of those guys were heavyweights. But he knocked out others as well. No one ever won that bet. Nobody ever beat Ernest Hemingway because [he] was big and strong, and he was in good shape, and he had been boxing from a young age. The people loved Hemingway and the boxing matches he had down here every week. The ring was just on the other side of the Government Dock. The dock has changed quite a bit since then, but four coconut trees were in the exact place where a ring should be —where posts should be. And Hemingway made the ring by strapping ropes off his boat — the *Pilar* — around the coconut trees. And they used a sail for the canvas. Spread it right on top of the ground. And every Sunday they had boxing matches, and the whole island would be down there to watch these matches between Hemingway and some native. It always drew a big crowd.

Hemingway referenced the Knapp fight in a July 30, 1935, letter to Scribner's editor Max Perkins claiming that since the event, every islander wanted to meet him in the ring, especially after they had taken a drink or two for courage. Hemingway told Perkins he had "knocked them all out (so far!)," including a Biminite who was rumored to be the toughest man around. Fishing guide "Bonefish Willie" Duncombe said that once Hemingway was ready for his knockout punch, "He'd hit them and they'd fall like dead men" (Craig Davis). In Tim McDonald's "On Bimini, Bell Tolls for Hemingway's Legend," Sir Michael Checkley explains Biminites were impressed with the author's "strength, the way he carried himself — the boxing, the drinking and the fishing." For the current islanders, these stories are very much alive, and hearing them told from various perspectives allows the listener to understand why Hemingway was and is so admired. He did not just come to keep to himself and fish like so many of the ultra-wealthy anglers of his day. He made it a point to be out among the people and engaging with them, and these stories illustrate how much fun he had doing it.

Hemingway boxed with the natives on the Bimini dock in 1935.

Considering his profession, Hemingway assuredly was using his interactions with the natives as creative fodder for his fiction. Natty Saunders, for instance, claims to be the basis of Santiago in *The Old Man and the Sea*, suggesting the widespread belief that Gregorio Fuentes was Santiago's real-life counterpart is not true. Various other islanders corroborate his claim. Hilary Hemingway suggests that the most valuable information Hemingway gathered to write the fight scenes in the novel came from Carlos Gutiérrez in Cuba. The biographical connections between Hemingway's characters and the correlating personalities and experiences of real people he knew have been well-documented by critics over the years, and I think it would be safe to argue that *everyone* — from Bimini to Key West to Havana — who makes such claims is probably at least partially right. *The Old Man and the Sea* was the final great novel that was waiting to come out of Hemingway and many of the things he saw and experienced found their way into the narrative.

The fishing life in Bimini could not put Hemingway's publishing obligations on hold, and the correspondence reveals he worked on numerous projects throughout his three summers there. It is known that he labored over *To Have and Have Not*, his novel of 1937, in Bimini. He also put the final touches on *Green Hills of Africa* while fishing on the island. Reynolds asserts, "Bimini in summer was a fisherman's dream and an editor's nightmare if the fisherman was Ernest Hemingway with a serialized book in production" (204). With such excitement going on around him in that amazing summer of 1935, it is a wonder Max Perkins was able to pull the author through the project at all. Hemingway penned numerous articles as a correspondent for *Esquire* from Bimini, including some specifically about his adventures on the island, such as "The President Vanquishes: A Bimini Letter" from July 1935. The article opens with the lovely image of Hemingway writing the piece from atop the *Pilar* under a huge moon in the middle of the night as his guests slept below. He seemed willing to sacrifice sleep to write at night for the reward of fishing during what probably should have been workdays. Into 1937, as his interest and involvement with the Spanish Civil War increased, he worked on the documentary *The Spanish Earth* and a *Life* magazine article about Spain while in Bimini as well.

The Sharks and the Tommy Gun

In Hemingway's "Marlin off Cuba" in *American Big Game Fishing*, Hemingway warned the reader in no uncertain terms to avoid swimming on the northern shore of the island because the sharks were ravenously hungry due to a lack of feeder fish (80). I have seen too many large fins in the water to just jump in the ocean willy-nilly, but it is always wise to heed the advice of fishermen, as they are more aware of what is in the water than anyone else. During this time of inadequate tackle, technique really won the day. Hemingway came to Bimini having secured a complete education about sharks in Cuba. He was well aware of the particular challenges they posed for big-game anglers. Hemingway wrote of fishing for marlin in Cuba in "The Great Blue River" for *Holiday* magazine in 1949 that the angler had the option of letting the fish run with a loose drag, a strategy that usually enabled the sharks to eventually catch and maul the fish. Hemingway's preference was "for the angler [to] never rest" because that allowed respite for the fish, which would prolong the battle and bring the sharks into the mix (95). In describing the time he spent in Bimini with Hemingway in 1935, John Dos Passos explained to Tom Kemp in an article for *The Fisherman* that the sharks were such an annoyance that "they even bothered us bathing on the beach," in addition to giving the fishermen fits by "cutting off [. . .] hooked fish" at the end of the fight (84). Hemingway's relationship with sharks grew to legendary proportions during the summer of 1935, mainly because of the gift of a very rich angler.

The story goes that in May, Bill Leeds, who was in the area fishing at the same time as Hemingway, gave the author a Thompson submachine gun that Leeds had kept on his own boat. Dos Passos, who was along for this particular ride, alleged Hemingway worked very hard to persuade Leeds to part with his weapon: "He'd been trying all sorts of expedients over the rum Collinses to get William B.

Leeds to part with his submachine gun," including games of chance and contests of skill (65). Somehow, Leeds was induced to hand over the gun to the author. Afterward, Hemingway always stored the weapon on the *Pilar* wherever he fished. (Humorously, at the end of "He Who Gets Slap Happy," he insisted the weapon "never comes into the U.S." because it is housed by a friend who lives out of the country [182].) The sight of a very famous man shooting into the water with a submachine gun in the tropics had to be curious, so it is no wonder that a great body of stories emerged from these incidents.

Hemingway used the famous Thompson submachine gun in Bimini in 1937, two years after he obtained it from William B. Leeds.

Hemingway himself acknowledged to fellow writer Sara Murphy in a July 1935 letter, "We shoot sharks with it [the Thompson submachine gun]. Shot 17 in two weeks. All over ten feet long. As soon as they put their heads out we give them a burst" (Day 7). He also wrote candidly of his use of the weapon to kill sharks in *Esquire*. Plenty of other folks who fished with Hemingway have unreal stories to tell about the things they saw. Reiger's *Profiles in Saltwater Angling* includes an interview with famed angler Johnny Cass, who explained the big sharks in Bimini used to get into schools of other fish and just wait with their mouths open for one to make its fatal leap. Cass and crew would "cruise up to those monsters and pour lead down their throats from machine guns. Sharks don't seem to wait around with their heads out of the water over there anymore (329)!"

In May 1935, the infamous tommy gun played a role in an incident involving Mike Strater and the storied 1,000-pound marlin. Hemingway was on the boat with Strater, and while his pal fought the fish, Hemingway attempted to keep the sharks at bay with his gun.

Mike Lerner and Hemingway take target practice in Bimini in 1937.
Oh, to be a pelican on the dock that day.

Strater felt Hemingway's action actually put more blood in the water and attracted the sharks, leading to the loss of what would have been his greatest catch and resulting in hard feelings. Even the apple-cored marlin still weighed 500 pounds, but that was no consolation for Strater. Judging by his future behavior with the weapon, Hemingway likely did not see any error in his handling of the situation, and Day writes that "despite his treatment of Strater, Hemingway did have a sense of fair play and responsibility" (8). The author wrote up his version of the day's events in "The President Vanquishes" for *Esquire* shortly after the experience, but the tommy gun was notably absent from the narrative. While Strater's fish was a total loss, what the author gained, Hilary Hemingway argues, was creative fuel for his later fiction. She says, "You could make a strong argument that the shark attack on Mike Strater's marlin was important for Ernest to visualize the attack on Santiago's great prize" in *The Old Man and the Sea*.

For the 21st-century reader, these tales paint Hemingway as a horribly cruel man who took pleasure in killing animals for fun — and not in a sporting context. Much like Hemingway's bull-fighting fiction (which I cannot bear to read), the descriptions of him dying the ocean red with shark blood turn my stomach. Even though shark populations at that historical juncture were not in danger of extinction and the modern concept of conservation had not been coined then, the stories involving the sharks and the tommy gun are cringe-worthy. It does not dissuade me that these sharks were killed in defense of game fish. Hemingway did not find himself in the position of the fictional Santiago, battling life and death while killing sharks bare-handed with only makeshift tools in an effort to bring his great marlin home. Santiago needed that fish to pay for his next meal; Hemingway did not need these game fish to survive. Interpreting these events through my 21st-century lens makes it difficult to absolutely reconcile them with Hemingway's conservationist and sportsmanlike qualities that will be discussed later. Like the day when he managed to shoot himself in both legs on the *Pilar*, the tommy gun tales remind us that he was just as human and flawed as the rest of us. The fault is ours — not his — when we build up his biography to fantastical proportions.

Beyond the incredible fishing records, the "Big Fat Slob" incident, the boxing, and the tommy gun tales, talking to the natives reveals the joy Hemingway brought to the people. It must have been a blast to have him around during those incredible summers. Thomas Saunders says Hemingway loved a good cookout, and "all the fish he caught, he barbequed or roasted on the beach and invited the natives to participate and celebrate." Ansil Saunders remembers the young people loved him especially because "he was very liberal with money. The young boys on Bimini looked forward to when he would come. He would play 'scramble money' with them, throwing quarters into the ocean for them to find." Nothing has been said so far in this book

Artist Thomas Saunders displays one of his lovely pieces modeled after the events of *The Old Man and the Sea*. He is an enchanting storyteller, my favorite on the island.

of Hemingway's drinking, but he lived it up in Bimini as he did in so many other places. Thomas recollects that when the author would walk down to go fishing, "he'd have three things: a machine gun, a fishing pole, and a 40-ounce bottle of rum. Sometimes people would come and say to my grandfather (he was the police, he was the constable) – 'There's a man walking down the road. He has a machine gun and a bottle of rum, and he's drunk.' And he'd say, 'Don't bother him. That's Ernest Hemingway. He's crazy.' So nobody bothered him." On an island where time moves very slowly, the fast-paced Hemingway spectacle had to be like the best circus coming to town.

The Bimini Chronology

It is most surprising that, for someone who had such a profound impact on the island of Bimini, Hemingway actually did not spend as much continuous time there as one might expect. Brewster Chamberlin's marvelous *The Hemingway Log: A Chronology of His Life and Times* collates all the evidence available about Hemingway's day-to-day locations and activities. Each time I reach for Chamberlin's work to confirm a date or detail, I wonder how Hemingway scholars managed before its publication. After his Key West departure for Bimini on April 15, 1935, Hemingway remained on the island until May 31, when he flew by seaplane with Pauline from Cat Cay to Miami on the way back to Key West (159). In a June 3, 1935, letter to Jane Mason written from Key West, he confirmed he "left the boat at Bimini." Hemingway and Carlos Gutiérrez flew back to Cat Cay by seaplane and took a ferry over to Bimini on June 7 (160). Hemingway's two youngest boys then flew with Pauline on June 24 (161). Hemingway and Pauline left Bimini for Key West on August 14 in the *Pilar* (161). For the year 1935, the documented evidence places Hemingway on the island for 115 days.

Hemingway's time in Bimini in 1936 was shorter than he enjoyed the previous year. On June 4, 1936, he piloted the *Pilar* with

Pauline and all three boys to Bimini (167). Pauline returned to Key West early that summer with her two sons, leaving Jack on the island with Ernest. Hemingway and his oldest son returned to Key West on the *Pilar* on July 18 (169). The summer of 1936 was arguably the pinnacle of Bimini's glory days as 37 marlin (ranging from just under 200 to just over 700 pounds) were boated in a four-week timespan (Thornton). Hemingway's contribution to the tally was a fish weighing 542 pounds. For the whole year of 1936, he was on the island for a total of 45 documented days.

In the spring of 1937, Hemingway began writing his Spanish Civil War cables, likely realizing this was the kind of work one cannot complete from afar. He made a few Bimini fishing runs in 1937, though most critics until Chamberlin suggested that he only made

Artist and writer Lynn Bogue Hunt, Tommy Shevlin, Captain Bill Fagen, and Ernest Hemingway inspect a 636-pound blue marlin. Hunt, a 1998 IGFA Hall of Fame inductee, designed the original logo for the organization.

one very short trip of a handful of days in 1937. On May 26, 1937, he departed from Key West on the *Pilar* and went to Bimini (187). Pauline and her boys made the trip by seaplane. Hemingway left the island on June 3 by airplane for New York to deliver a speech at a meeting of the League of American Writers (187). He flew back to Cat Cay on June 22, staying until July 6, when he flew to New York again (188). There is evidence Hemingway was in Key West on July 15 and back in Bimini by July 21 (189). The last letter he wrote from Bimini as far as we know was on July 27, 1937, to the American painter Waldo Peirce. Hemingway departed the island for what many feel was the last time on August 2, 1937 (190). Therefore, he was in Bimini in 1937 for three trips totaling 37 days.

The reduced time Hemingway had to devote to fishing in Bimini during these years (115 days in 1935, 45 days in 1936, and 37 days in 1937) is significant. For reasons that will be examined at length in Chapter V, it became clear Hemingway no longer had the extended time and energy to devote to the kind of uninterrupted fishing effort that he found fulfilling. The unbelievable part of the story is that a span of 197 days spread out over three summers could have such a

The Hemingway Bimini Summers

1935:
April 15–May 31: 46 days
June 7–August 14: 69 days

1936:
June 4–July 18: 45 days

1937:
May 26–June 3: 9 days
June 22–July 6: 15 days
July 21–August 2: 13 days

crucial impact on a place. Even more astounding is that he never even lived there permanently. Can you imagine spending fewer than 200 days on an island and having a scholar 80 years later write a whole book about how you influenced the history of the location? Volumes have been published about Hemingway as a literary celebrity, of his incredible ability to command the attention of the public simply by traveling to a new locale or learning (and inevitably mastering) a new sport. The fame he garnered in Bimini from 1935 to 1937 had absolutely nothing to do with his fiction. Aside from a few articles about the island, he had not published any major work about Bimini up to that point. His unfinished Bimini manuscript would not be released until well after his death, and he did not even begin working on it until the fall of 1945.

The description of the years 1935, 1936, and 1937 as "Camelot" in this chapter's title was no exaggeration. All of the sport's luminaries were in position and Bimini was their dazzling stage. Hemingway was on an absolute fishing tear, with Norman German pointing out in 1935 alone, "he won every tournament in the Key West-Havana-Bimini triangle, besting notables like Michael Lerner and Kip Farrington." His enthusiasm oozed as he described to Max Perkins the current fishing situation in Bimini in the July 30, 1935, letter. He chronicled the days and the fish he caught, ranging from 200 to 500 pounds, with sometimes more than one massive catch in a day. Ansil Saunders, who was born in 1932, says he can remember seeing "as many as six billfish and four tuna hanging up on the scaffolding on Lerner's property once. Lerner buried the carcasses and used them to make manure for the garden." Saunders claimed, "I saw 46 tuna on the Big Game Club dock in one day, and there were others on different docks that day, too." He says, "Some days in June, it looks like you could walk from here to Miami on the backs of the tuna." While it seems preposterous, Farrington claimed Bimini anglers in those days sometimes even hooked two fish simultaneously, especially during mating season, a time when "Hemingway and Lerner [. . .] lost some of their best fish when the smaller and more active fish cut the larger one off" (*Atlantic Game Fishing* 209). Bimini was destined to become "The Fishing Capital of the World," and I sure am glad its discovery

A very happy Hemingway shows off a Bimini tuna in 1937. This fish, weighing 319 pounds and boated in 48 minutes, was actually the second unmutilated tuna Hemingway hooked in the summer of 1935. This photograph appeared in the August 1935 edition of *Esquire* with the article "He Who Gets Slap Happy: A Bimini Letter."

was delayed until Hemingway, Lerner, Farrington, and Heilner could get there to do the honors.

In "Fishing at Bimini" in 1935, Farrington made an audacious prediction. After naming the nautical landmarks and smaller islands that comprise Bimini, he said, "Memorize the names now as you will often hear more of them in the years to come, particularly if you are a fisherman" (109). Farrington's forecast was exactly right, and I argue the main catalysts that made it so were Hemingway's arrival in Bimini and his subsequent meeting with Mike Lerner. As we will see in the next chapter, their friendship resulted in much more than just fame for either angler or for the magnificent waters of Bimini.

"There is enough sport in the waters surrounding the Bimini
Islands to keep any angler young for years."

— Hal Hennesey, "Exploring the Bahamas: Part One"

IV

The Early Fishing Clubs and the Emergence of the IGFA

It is fitting that Hemingway would play such an integral role in the development of the most important organization for the sport of big-game fishing. After all, he owned his first fishing rod by age two, and he joined his local branch of the Louis Agassiz Club, a nature study group, by the age of four. The story of the International Game Fish Association begins well before Hemingway's fishing years, and without question, the most authoritative source about the group's inception is Mike Rivkin's spectacular *Big-Game Fishing Headquarters: A History of the IGFA*. Because its only printing in 2005 consisted of 900 copies, it is an expensive book, but it is well worth the price. Rivkin's storytelling ability makes it one of the best nonfiction books I have ever had the pleasure of reading.

The end of the 19th and the turn of the 20th century was really the time when anglers began to take notice of big-game species and to consider catching them as a sport (Rivkin 16). Fishing clubs existed well before the formation of the IGFA. Rivkin credits Charles Holder's 1898 capture of a 183-pound tuna for "set[ting] the stage for the formation of the world's first big-game fishing organization: The Tuna Club of Santa Catalina Island" in California (19). Holder is also noted in the history books for a conservationist mindset that was many decades ahead of its time. Because the gear and tackle anglers needed to pursue big game had not been developed yet (much less perfected), the conditions the anglers faced can only be characterized as brutal. Philip Wylie, a former IGFA Vice President, published a 1952 *Esquire* supplement that perfectly characterized the kind of anglers who started the early fishing clubs and were willing to face challenges too numerous to count on their quest to land big fish. The picture he painted was not for the faint of heart: "Standing in open boats, [...] — with reel handles which *spun backwards* whenever a hooked fish ran and no more 'drag' than could be exerted by thumb-pressure on a leather tab against the line spool — these sportsmen caught tuna, marlin, broadbill swordfish and other rugged giants of the blue waters. They came home with bloodied hands, busted knuckles, broken fingers [...] and only occasionally with a fish" (63). In those days, the fishermen willing to make the physical sacrifice to pursue the sport did so out of pure devotion to angling and a refusal to ever back down from even the most insurmountable challenge.

The Salt Water Anglers of America

As Hemingway's angling skill grew and his network of friends in the fishing fraternity expanded, his involvement with the organizations attempting to govern the sport increased. The Salt Water Anglers of America was in existence at least by 1934. The introduction of the 1935 first edition of Eugene Connett's *American Big Game Fishing* was written by Mrs. Oliver C. Grinnell, who at the time was the president of the SWAA. Grinnell mentions an October 27, 1930, column in the *Miami Herald* by Erl Roman that "pleaded [...] for anglers to affiliate and to agree upon and adopt some set rules and specifications and ethics so that an angler from any part of the world might establish a record that would be recognized and go down in history *as* a record" (xiv–xv). She goes on to explain that Roman's column put enough pressure on the SWAA, which was headquartered in New York City, for the group to agree to promote a set of standards. (The goals and focus of the SWAA can be examined in the organization's mission statement from 1935, printed on the next page.) Archival evidence at the American Museum of Natural History reveals the SWAA membership was working closely with the AMNH. In fact, a February 11, 1935, letter from AMNH's Vice-Director W. M. Faunce to the SWAA treasurer acknowledges the museum had agreed to let the group use its facility as a meeting space (Central Archives, 1267, AMNH). Just two days later, a letter from Van Campen Heilner, who was the guest speaker for that month's SWAA meeting, wrote to Faunce and commented on the "tremendous attendance" for the event which gave him "great difficulty getting inside the doors in order to speak" (February 13, 1935, Central Archives, 1267, AMNH). The SWAA was apparently a robust organization at that time because Heilner alludes to the fact that 700 people had to be turned away at the door due to lack of space.

A few months later in 1935, Hemingway's path crossed the SWAA trajectory. On the same day — August 29, 1935 — two letters were mailed to Hemingway, one from Grinnell and one from Erl Roman. The gist of the letters makes it appear that Grinnell and Roman wrote Hemingway in concert with one another. Roman's letter reveals that since the last time he saw Hemingway in Bimini (which would have only been a few months previously), the author had expressed interest in joining the SWAA and had suggested to Roman several modifications to the group's approach. Roman also told Hemingway that at an organizational meeting on the previous night, the membership voted unanimously to appoint Hemingway to the executive board and to the post of first vice president. Roman reminded Hemingway that the SWAA is "comprised of a mighty fine

B*elieving that the perpetuation of the sport of salt-water angling in America calls for the unified action of individual anglers and anglers' associations all over the country, there has been organized:*

Salt Water Anglers of America

a national association dedicated to the conservation of salt water fishes and the promotion of sportsmanlike methods of angling. The purposes of this organization shall be:

[1] To AFFILIATE and cooperate with existing local salt-water angling clubs in all matters pertaining to the improvement of angling conditions in the coastal and off-shore waters of the Atlantic and Pacific oceans.

[2] To LEND every possible support and assistance to groups organizing new salt water angling clubs.

[3] To ESTABLISH local representatives all along the Atlantic and Pacific coasts for the dissemination of information of interest to the salt water angler.

[4] To ESTABLISH uniform regulations governing salt water angling in this country and to establish standard tackle regulations.

[5] To PROMOTE conservation by the encouragement of the use of light tackle.

[6] To WORK in conjunction with local clubs, state conservation departments, and the federal government in designing and presenting legislation to discourage the slaughter, by any means, of salt water fish, and to improve salt water angling conditions in every way.

[7] To WORK with existing agencies in establishing an authoritative listing of all American salt-water fishing records.

[8] By EDUCATION and other means to elevate salt-water angling to a higher plane of sportsmanship.

This document from the American Museum of Natural History Library announces the mission of the Salt Water Anglers of America in 1935.

lot of sportsmen and the organization can do a great deal of good in a practical way. It cannot do this, however, without the aid of good practical fishermen" such as the author. Grinnell's letter of the same day accepted Hemingway's SWAA application and welcomed him to the group. She explained her impending retirement from the presidency and that the current vice president, C. Blackburn Miller, would be taking over. Included in Grinnell's letter was a current listing of the executive board, which, interestingly, included Mike Lerner at the time. If he accepted the role, Grinnell insisted, she planned to appoint Hemingway to a significant committee. He responded to Grinnell in September of 1935, accepting the invitation to the vice presidency and writing, "Delighted [to] serve saltwater anglers in any capacity." He then apologized for his late response due to the devastation in the Florida Keys from the 1935 Labor Day Hurricane. It is unclear what Hemingway may have done for the organization or how long the terms of service lasted for officers. One source suggested Hemingway actually became president of the Salt Water Anglers of America, but I was unable to confirm that with any other research.

On May 7, 1936, Lerner informed Hemingway he had sent Grinnell a letter to resign from the Tackle Committee, though not from the SWAA as a whole. The letter includes a fascinating snapshot of the state of big-game fishing in that precise moment. In it, Lerner advocated for giving the companies that design and produce tackle the freedom to innovate without the constrictions of rigorous specifications from the fishing clubs. Additionally, he championed that beyond the standard tackle specifications, an unrestricted category should be added to provide inclusion for the anglers who were experimenting in virgin waters and experiencing unexpected obstacles that required troubleshooting.

As big-game fishermen started spreading out on the globe in search of greater adventures, and as pictorial evidence of their amazing conquests reached newspapers and magazines, fishing as a sport became a recognized mainstream pursuit and began to grow exponentially. All of the reasons and conditions cited in previous chapters had an influence on the development of the sport, but the sensational writing of the early pioneers and ambassadors of big-game fishing, who had the skill to fish well and then write about it in such an enticing way, was the driving force that enabled its worldwide expansion. Likewise, because most of the anglers who were driving the sport and writing about it were in Bimini in the 1930s, it makes perfect sense that the precursor club to the IGFA was formed there. The genesis for the idea first appears in a letter from Hemingway to Lerner in June 1936. Mrs. Grinnell was in Bimini at that time, and on the whole, Hemingway appeared to like her. He also communicated an informal proposal for a "humble" fishing organization yet to emerge. Admission credentials would require anglers to have fairly landed a blue marlin or a tuna in excess of 400 pounds.

The Bahamas Marlin and Tuna Club

After the sparkling summer of 1935 when Bimini emerged as the

"Sport Fishing Capital of the World," the formation of the Bahamas Marlin and Tuna Club followed on November 23, 1936. Watson notes a meeting was held at the home of Tommy and Lorraine Shevlin (139). In attendance were Hemingway, Lerner, T. Shevlin, Anthony Baldridge, Farrington, Julio Sanchez, and Roman (Chamberlin 173). Hemingway was elected president, Lerner, Shevlin, and Baldridge were vice presidents, Sanchez was treasurer, Farrington was the secretary, and Roman was the historian. In *Atlantic Game Fishing*, Farrington outlined the finalized rules of acceptance for the new club:

> Gentlemen anglers who have caught a marlin, tuna, or mako weighing over four hundred pounds, and lady anglers who have hung either of these fish weighing over three hundred pounds will be admitted, if the fish have been caught in Bimini waters. Affidavits specifying how their fish were caught are to be signed by boat captains and anglers. The aims of the club are: To keep the fishing at Bimini on a sportsmanlike basis; to build a smokehouse for the disposal of the big marlin and tuna, so that the meat the natives do not eat will not be wasted; and to encourage scientists in their study of the marlin. (237)

From these goals, you can see how equity, conservation, and scientific inquiry were at the center of the club's mission. One of the innovative ideas Lerner and Hemingway had about the club was to train and certify the Bimini fishing guides in the angling specifications of the BMTC. The certified guides could prevent the unethical and rule-bending activities some of the guides in the area were attempting as the desire for records among their paying clients was immense.

At least one reporter had some journalistic fun at the BMTC's expense immediately after its formation. In an article called "New Big Fish Club Is Organized, But It's Awfully Hard to Crash" for the *N.Y.C. World-Telegram*, Ray Trullinger wrote, "Another new big fish anglers' association, the Bahamas Marlin and Tuna Club, has just bloomed in our midst, and, judging from the eligibility requirements, it doesn't appear the Membership Committee ever will be snowed under with applications." Trullinger had a point about the rigorous membership requirements, and a December 4, 1936, letter from Kip Farrington to Hemingway proves the group's leadership was cognizant of the tall order their requirements represented. Essentially, Farrington accounted for the tepid response to the club by New York reporters by rationalizing they simply could not fathom catching a fish of such size. After all, at the end of 1936, few people had enjoyed the experience of fishing in places like Bimini. Without this frame of reference, the skepticism about the BMTC's requirements made perfect sense.

It appears that in 1937, the group was still discussing and/or negotiating about specifications. Lerner wrote to Hemingway on August 19 that he was including copies of the British Tunny Club's rules. These guidelines, Lerner insisted, were as loose as any he had ever seen, and in light of the considerable demands on Bimini fishermen, the BMTC's guidelines should be perfectly acceptable. Lerner's letters to Hemingway reveal the foundational details of the BMTC as they were laid out. On January 4, 1938, Lerner wrote to explain an agreement had been reached between Wasey, Farrington, and Shevlin to construct a trophy room and club. Negotiations were also ongoing for the group's philosophy statement, regulations, scientific position, membership fees, and application process. The final piece of the puzzle not yet accounted for was the writing of the group's charter, a job Lerner placed at Hemingway's feet due to his obvious talents as a writer and an angler. In its infancy, the sport needed an ethical code to serve as a guiding beacon, and Lerner felt Hemingway was the one most qualified to compose the first draft. Oddly enough, even as these arrangements were being made, Lerner's letter suggested there may have been talk about possibly disbanding or discontinuing the BMTC.

The conch-lined gates of Brown's Marina. Conch shells are absolutely everywhere on North and South Bimini — on the beaches, piled outside of conch salad shacks, and worked into masonry.

There is not a lot of data available about the Bahamas Marlin and Tuna Club, so it is unclear how many meetings took place, how long the group stayed together, or what was accomplished. By March 1937, Hemingway was ready to resign as president. He wrote to Lerner on March 4 to inform him that the club decided to postpone voting on any tackle specifications until Lerner could be in attendance, a testament to Lerner's stature among his peers. Hemingway mentioned his intention to resign because he "can't be there to look after things now" due to various circumstances, including his work in the Spanish Civil War. The author proposed Lerner deserved to be the president because he is a "sportsman," a testament to their mutual admiration for one another.

Agreement among historians is that the Bahamas Marlin and Tuna Club was the beginning of what would become the IGFA just a few years later. Two of the goals of the BMTC were specific to Bimini: to develop ethical rules for fishing those waters and to build a smokehouse to reduce waste. Even if the club had achieved all of

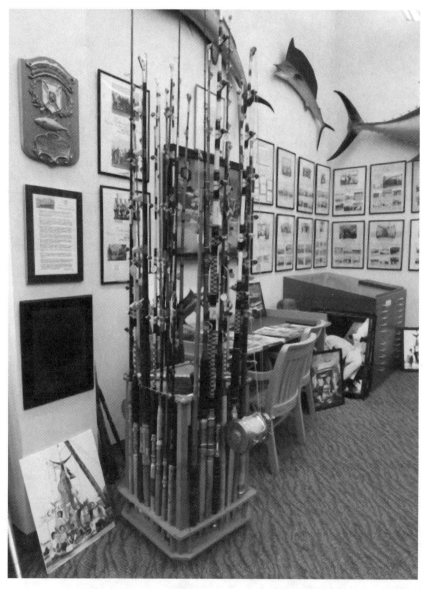

A collection of vintage rods is a highlight of the IGFA library.

its goals, it would not have addressed the larger problems facing the entire sport of big-game fishing worldwide. A different organization was still needed — one with enough prestige to govern fishing across the globe. Such an endeavor required the collaboration of a team of luminaries, not just one charismatic leader, and the group that had assembled as the BMTC was an excellent start.

The letters that passed between Hemingway and Lerner in the few years after the formation of the BMTC indicate their mutual dissatisfaction with the larger state of angling affairs. They were concerned about both fishing in Bimini and on the world stage, complaining about how certain innovations by those following big game had exceeded the bounds of reasonable sportsmanship, taking the excitement and skill out of the pursuit. It cannot be overstressed how alert they both were to the *sporting* component of fishing. It is the natural tendency of the history books to glorify the unbelievable pictures of the fishermen on the dock with the rack of magnificent prize fish hanging behind them. It is impossible for the photos to make the distinction between the sportsmen who followed a code of ethical conduct and the fishermen who used any means necessary (whether honorable or not) to boat their fish. Lerner felt that innovations such as installing the rod into the frame of the vessel would remove the sport from the endeavor, and he, Hemingway, and the other like-minded anglers in Bimini in those years understood the need for standards that would secure respect for the sport forever.

Hemingway and Lerner were looking well beyond Bimini as well. On April 2, 1937, Lerner sent Hemingway a letter in Spain while the author was covering the Civil War there. Lerner reiterated his reluctance to ever take on the leadership role in any angling organization because of his attempt to focus on his enjoyment of the sport instead of the business of it. The fragile state of the freshly born sport was his impetus for changing his position at this critical moment. Lerner explained what he saw as his moral obligation to see to it that the established angling rules were followed by all to preserve the health of the sport. Giving Hemingway credit for the initial idea to form the club, Lerner asked the author to stay at the helm until it could be birthed while promising his full monetary support. The entirety of this letter is important for a number of reasons, the main one being the shift in Lerner's rhetoric about the need for the worldwide organization. He could no longer stand by and watch as guidelines were disregarded and the sport floundered. Even though he insisted he did not want to be president, Lerner was clearly the best man at the time to take charge of the movement toward proper rules and regulations. Other letters from 1937 and 1938 echo Lerner's growing determination and his increasing willingness to assume leadership. For a number of personal and professional reasons that will be analyzed in future chapters, these were the precise years during which Hemingway was having to pull away from Bimini but was still fishing in earnest. In 1938, in fact, he caught seven marlin in one day, a world record (German). Lerner emerges in these letters as a clear

The beauty of the IGFA facility in Dania Beach, Florida, is magnificent at sunset.

leader, one who is already making plans and taking care of the minute details, of which there were many. He made financial arrangements, for instance, for the Bimini smokehouse (Incoming Correspondence, January 4, 1938, JFK). (Hemingway also donated $100 toward the project in 1937, though the correspondence reveals Lerner returned the funds when it was unclear if the project was on track. It does not appear the smokehouse was ever built.) In that message, Lerner continued to elucidate the need for a worldwide governing body with the necessary impact and reach that would ensure its effectiveness.

The IGFA Is Born

Lerner and Hemingway were not the only anglers who were in discussion about the need for such an organization. It was Lerner, with his acute mind for business networking, who began to reach out to members of the angling community to gather their thoughts and see if they felt one central body was even feasible. The responses Lerner received from anglers around the world were positive, so the decision to proceed with the International Game Fish Association was made. The first historic meeting took place at the American Museum of Natural History in New York City on June 7, 1939. The attendees were "[Dr. William] Gregory, Museum ichthyologists Francesca LaMonte and John Nichols, author Van Campen Heilner, and Lerner" (Rivkin 51). Hemingway was not at the first meeting. Rivkin distinguishes Lerner alone with the formation of the IGFA, which most scholars would agree is a fair statement. Dr. Gregory, who was the chair of Ichthyology and Comparative Anatomy Department at the AMNH, was elected as the first president, though Lerner took the position in 1940. Hemingway was selected as the group's first vice president, a title he held (later with additional vice presidents) until his death in 1961. Heilner was appointed to the Executive Committee of the IGFA. Lynn Bogue Hunt designed the organization's excellent logo. LaMonte, who collaborated with Hemingway and Lerner over many years and participated in field work across the globe on the AMNH's expeditions, served as the group's diligent secretary.

While Hemingway and Lerner had already worked together in the organization of the Bahamas Marlin and Tuna Club, the goals and overall scope of the IGFA were on a completely different level because they sought to govern a number of facets of sport fishing *on a worldwide scale*. The earliest aims of the IGFA were as follows: "create a portfolio of standardized angling rules along with a rigorous ethical credo, assume the responsibility of saltwater record-keeping from *Field & Stream* [which had been attempting to document global records up to that time], develop a network of International Representatives to promulgate IGFA principles in distant lands and [...] find a place to work" (Rivkin 57). The last goal was graciously covered by the AMNH, which opened office space to the IGFA, probably because Mike Lerner had agreed to cover *all* of the organization's financial expenses. His great generosity was not just extended for a few years; his belief in the need for the IGFA was so strong that he remained the chief financial contributor until he stepped down as president in 1961, 17 years before his death. John T. Nichols, the Curator of Recent Fishes at the AMNH wrote to museum director Roy C. Andrews on March 25, 1940, to tell Andrews about a conversation that had just transpired about the new IGFA. In the note, Nichols relayed what Lerner said about the organization's mission: "The general object [...] is to broaden the exchange of data between game-fishermen and the American Museum, to include other institutions of a like nature, and gamefishermen of the world instead of mostly local ones" (Central Archives, 1290.4, AMNH). This conversation with Nichols is just one illustration of Lerner's dedication to making the necessary connections the IGFA would need to survive. Lerner was a savvy organizer and good judge of character, and the personnel decisions he made in the early years of the IGFA contributed greatly to its success. Immediately after its formation, the IGFA had a good reputation, mainly because a great deal of planning and legwork had gone into the process before it was ever announced. When the public interfaced with the IGFA, they found themselves corresponding with well-respected scientists and some of the most skillful and well-known anglers in the world. In a letter to Hemingway from Lerner on July 13, 1943, Hemingway was praised for the various ways he was helping the museum with its work, including his continued project of scientific documentation. Hemingway's contribution, Lerner insisted, helped the IGFA fulfill its mission to marry scientific knowledge with sport fishing. The conception of this symbiotic union was the core of Lerner's genius in envisioning the organization. He knew the IGFA's sustainability hinged upon the right personnel and an intentional approach. The group's strategies for its press releases, major publications, and correspondence was well-organized and thorough, notwithstanding that the first five years of its existence were paralleled by World War II. By the time the war ended, the IGFA's refined mission was ready: "1. To encourage the study of game fishes for whatever purpose; 2. To set and maintain the highest standards

IGFA Headquarters

of ethics and create rules accordingly; 3. To encourage recreational angling and data accumulation surrounding same; and 4. To maintain a listing of world record catches" (Rivkin 66). From that point in time to the present, this is precisely what the IGFA has provided to the angling community.

The Question of Hemingway's Contribution

Some scholars minimalize Hemingway's actual aid to the IGFA in the form of direct service, and the correspondence seems to bear out their assertions. The reader sees in the letters the complete devotion of Mike Lerner to the IGFA; in contrast, Hemingway appears very interested but just not as actively involved. One of the main reasons for the disparity was that Hemingway was still writing for a living, and Lerner had the financial freedom to make the IGFA his work. Maybe it was not that Hemingway did not want to be so intimately involved but that he just no longer had the time to invest.

Several of Hemingway's letters to Lerner acknowledge in a roundabout way his decreasing level of involvement in the IGFA as the years passed. For instance, on August 2, 1943, Hemingway extolled Lerner for the quality of the recently released IGFA annual publication. The letter demonstrates Hemingway felt regret that he "didn't do more to help with it." He pledged to "go to bat" and really invest more effort on behalf of the organization after the conclusion of World War II. The research does not reveal any evidence to suggest Hemingway kept his promise, though in fairness it is quite possible significant additional contributions were made that no one could locate now.

Hilary Hemingway offers additional context important to the discussion of her uncle's contributions to the IGFA. She says, "You can see in his letters that Ernest admired the hell out of Mike's fishing skills — and honestly all the great science work he was funding with the American Museum of Natural History and the many fishing expeditions with Francesca LaMonte. It was what Ernest himself had aspired to do when he set off with the *Scientificos* in 1934. Only Mike Lerner took it to a whole new level." She went on to propose that Lerner's demonstrated excellence in the management of the IGFA may have cooled Hemingway's ambitions: "We know Ernest was a competitive fellow, but what Mike Lerner was able to do, not just with the AMNH, but with founding the IGFA as well, there was no way to compete, and I don't think Ernest's heart was in it — in part because Ernest loved and respected Lerner and in part because he himself was falling out of love with the rich boys who were doing all

A bust of Mike Lerner is on display at IGFA headquarters.

the big-game fishing." Two close pals coleading such an ambitious operation could certainly put the friendship in peril, and perhaps Hemingway realized the danger and retreated for the sake of the relationship. Hemingway's displeasure with the attitudes and behaviors of the rich are well-documented. In the late 1930s and '40s, the

An angler's dream: seemingly every book ever written about fishing is housed in the IGFA collection.

Bahamas and Florida were ground zero for fishermen, but Cuba to a degree remained insulated from this crowd, likely due to political unrest. This explanation would certainly make a lot of sense considering Hemingway's abandonment of both Bimini and Key West to fish Cuban waters almost exclusively in his later years.

Even the historians who downplay Hemingway's contributions to the actual business of the IGFA still acknowledge the great value he added in a number of other ways. Rivkin thinks Hemingway's major contributions came from his fishing articles about ethical behavior and his discussions with Lerner as the initial concept of the group was forming (69). The history books will never show how involved Hemingway was in the earliest conception of the organization; my guess is that he was at least an equal contributor in the brainstorming with Lerner. It can be argued those early years of the 1930s were when Hemingway was at the peak of his fishing prowess and the most plugged in to the evolving sport; therefore, I would categorize his input to Lerner's idea as incredibly significant.

Hemingway's willingness to lend his name and persona to the IGFA is another contribution that should not be underestimated. Jason Schratwieser, the Conservation Director for the IGFA, says

> Hemingway was huge [. . .] when he came on board in the very infancy of the IGFA. To have such a luminary figure but also someone who had sport-fishing chops was amazing. The IGFA was lucky. [He was already] a big literary figure, but he also had the gaming skills — he knew how to fish. So having that combination of somebody who knew how to fish and somebody who could write about it was very potent. In addition, there were a variety of conditions that in fact helped the IGFA. Lerner's vision of not just using this as a sport but saying that we can use fishing to help scientists get

data, teaming up with scientists early on, having a scientist as our first president — all of this was important. These things [. . .] helped catapult the IGFA to becoming the premier sport-fishing organization of the world.

Consider how many readers came to Hemingway's fiction because of the glamorous public persona propagated by the fabulous magazine articles about his fishing exploits and his travels. Think about how many people still pay $13.00 to visit Hemingway's Key West house each year although they likely know very little or maybe even nothing about his writing. It would naturally follow that interest in the IGFA (both in the past and the present) would increase due to its historical connections to Hemingway.

Hemingway as Conservationist

Based on some of the pictures included in this volume to this point and some of the fishing stories that have been told so far, the subheading "Hemingway as Conservationist" may seem like a bit of a misnomer. However, when one thoroughly considers *all* Hemingway wrote about fishing, his desire to gather knowledge about unknown species, his belief that game fish should be treated as humanely as possible, and his interest in preserving species situated him very much ahead of the curve in terms of conservation. Species preservation in the angling world is not a later 20th-century invention as one might suspect. Rivkin notes "a conservation ethic" with regard to tarpon in the late 1800s that helped save the population of that species once they were discovered as sporting fish (15). Early pioneers such as Lee Wulff, one of the first advocates of *catch and release*, dedicated his life to convincing anglers across the globe that "game fish are too valuable to be caught only once" ("Lee Wulff"). However, Schratwieser contends the term *catch and release* would not have been a phrase in Hemingway's vocabulary, explaining that in those years, most people "did not think casual angling could affect fish population." While these early sportsmen might not have known to be concerned about the impact of overfishing on species population, there is plenty of written evidence to suggest they were cognizant of (and bothered by) the waste of thousands of pounds of rotting game fish carcasses. In Heilner's 1937 *Salt Water Fishing*, he wrote with great passion about his disgust for the sight of mass numbers of dead sailfish, calling the slaughter "a shameful waste of this glorious creature. Anglers *must* be educated to releasing any and all fish that are uninjured and to keep *only* those individuals that are to be used for food or especially desired for mounting. To do otherwise is not only distinctly bad sportsmanship but stamps the angler as one who is ignorant of the fundamental principles of the game" (106). Later on that page, Heilner describes the hypothetical hooking of a great sailfish, his narrative reminding the reader that his or her enjoyment of the experience is not necessarily enhanced by the death of the creature. Heilner managed to articulate the conservationist mentality in terms a 1930s audience of big-game anglers could relate to: "'[H]e who fights and gets away will live to fight another day.' From releasing fish have come my greatest angling thrills" (107). These statements sound like contemporary rhetoric, yet amazingly they were first published in 1937.

The tide had turned in Mike Lerner's mind toward a conservation ideology as well in the 1930s. He explained in a letter to Hemingway on May 22, 1937, that it was time for people in Bimini to realize big-game catches need to be released when it seems the fish have a reasonable chance of survival after the battle is over. Going forward, Lerner said he was going to enjoy the challenge of catching them and then cut the line. The idea of these dazzling creatures swimming free was preferable to the sickening sight of them decomposing on a fish rack. This transition in Lerner's thinking is striking as he was a big-game hunter who went to great expense to go on safari and display his treasured trophies.

Hemingway was known to release big-game catches, too. German writes, "Hemingway's interest in pressuring big fish was partly founded on sympathy. An exhausted fish was more likely to be attacked by sharks and less likely to survive if released — and he released plenty at a time when it was not a moral imperative to do so." Discovering such early references to the question of species sustainability was quite startling and instilled in me a newfound respect for the innovative thinking that went beyond just the tackle, gear, and technique — and beyond these anglers and their own sporting good time. When properly contextualized, the strides men such as Heilner, Lerner, and Hemingway made in their thinking were tremendous, showing the reader just how visionary they truly were.

Remember Hemingway was among the anglers of the Bahamas Marlin and Tuna Club who joined together in 1936 with a goal of creating a smokehouse to prevent the waste of fish. Reiger offers an appraisal of the situation that puts the need for the smokehouse in perfect context: "By the time the Cat Cay Tournament began in 1939, there were objections [...] about the 'conspicuous consumption' of such a great resource. Some 42 anglers brought in 93,000 pounds of tuna, all of which were used for shark bait or otherwise wasted" (260). The idea of 93,000 pounds of fresh tuna rotting away is a tragedy; however, these anglers did not fully understand how their actions could lead to population decline and ultimately risk extinction for these game species. For a frame of reference, think about the unethical practices that are ongoing today, such as blatant commercial overfishing, the cruel practice shark finning in Asia, and the disgraceful oceanic pollution. These fishermen *know* they are endangering troubled species and engaging in cruel and destructive practices, and they simply do not care.

Plenty of critics have taken an opposing stance to my position, claiming Hemingway's actions are inconsistent with his purported philosophy. In "The President Vanquishes," Hemingway criticized the rotting game fish in Bimini by describing how these fish are "wasted scandalously" in a "disgusting" and "sickening" display (167). He went on to write, "Killing fish for no useful purpose, or allowing their meat to waste, wantonly, should be an offense punishable by law" (167). Reynolds pounces on this statement, claiming the author's comments

Hemingway and Carlos Gutiérrez show off the day's prize in Bimini in 1935: a 12-foot marlin.

in his piece were a feeble attempt to "ease his conscience" and deflect responsibility for the wastefulness away from himself (206). Instead of assessing Hemingway's remarks for a theoretical motive, I choose to focus on the remarkable fact that he was beginning to actually *think* about the results of his sporting actions — in 1935 no less. I am not proposing that history should give Hemingway and his fishing colleagues a pass for their behaviors, but I do think they should be assessed based on what was known about species conservation during their time. As we have seen in the case of Hemingway and Lerner, they actively pursued the scientific knowledge that ultimately led us to our conception of marine conservation today, and what we know about the field of conservation is constantly changing. The Endangered Species Preservation Act was not put into law until 1966 (five years after Hemingway's death), and the term *endangered* was not defined specifically until the Endangered Species Act of 1973. Since then, there have been amendments in 1978, 1982, 1988, and 2004 as our own knowledge evolves and as species populations change. In a perfect world, fishing practices (particularly commercial activities) would also change at the same pace as our expansion of knowledge about the plight of endangered species. Unfortunately, we are facing an uphill battle, and organizations such as the IGFA are essential if we hope to preserve the great resources of the ocean.

In Hemingway's writing about fishing, the reader observes his concern as well for the most humane treatment of the hooked game fish. Now, I am not suggesting Hemingway was an animal welfare advocate. He dearly loved his pets, but he killed *a lot* of fish and other big game for sport in his lifetime. The way German contextualizes Hemingway's sporting activities is spot-on: "Asking him to be an animal-rights activist in 1940 would be like asking Buffalo Bill to be a vegetarian." What Hemingway did, though, was demonstrate a very early regard for the humane death of the game fish. In "Marlin off

Cuba," he described angling as "a sport in which a man or woman seeks to kill or capture a fish by the means which will afford the fisherman the greatest pleasure and best demonstrate the speed, strength and leaping ability of the fish," a creature which should then be killed "as promptly as possible [...] and as mercifully as possible" (70). Here Hemingway addressed the suffering of the injured animal and argued sportsmen should avoid wounding but not killing an animal. He advocated killing the fish "quickly" and "mercifully," and he was willing, in what amounts to a Cuban fishing primer for aspiring anglers, to encourage them to treat game fish as humanely as possible. In his article "The Great Blue River" for *Holiday* magazine, he offered similar guidelines for handling big game in Cuba, instructing the fisherman to avoid hurting the animal during the fight and then to "club [the fish] for kindness" (95). Clubbing a fish "for kindness" might seem like an oxymoron, but when one considers the year in which this writing was published (1934 and 1949, respectively), it becomes clear these sentiments were profoundly important and should be included in any biographical consideration of Hemingway's character. In these pieces, he was taking a very public stand for a humane approach to a sport whose contests usually end in the death of the opponent. Many critics in my field over the past 40 years have seemed to be on a vendetta against Hemingway, vilifying his life and criticizing him at every turn, very often for faults that resulted from his being a product of his time period. Without providing historical and cultural context when biographical attacks are launched, the critic acts as unethically as he or she asserts Hemingway was.

If my appraisal of Hemingway's humane position did not persuade you, take it from Fidel Castro. In his autobiography *Fidel Castro: My Life*, the Cuban dictator claimed, "If Hemingway had lived a few years longer, I'd have liked to have time to talk much more with him. To become a little closer friends. [...] As a person, in the little

I knew him, he seemed to me, in his habits, his practices, his things, a very humane person" (Castro and Ramonet 592–593). So, if Fidel says you are humane, well then . . .

Women as Equal Competitors

You will recall from the previous section the quote from Hemingway's "Marlin off Cuba" that big-game fishing is "a sport in which a man *or woman* seeks to kill or capture a fish" (emphasis mine). It must be noted that he was using inclusive language in referring to big-game sportsmanship in the year 1934. Similarly, in the introduction Hemingway wrote for Farrington's 1937 *Atlantic Game Fishing*, he characterized big-game fishing as "a contest of strength and endurance between a man *or woman* and an over-sized fish" (10, emphasis mine). These quotations and many others reveal that Hemingway viewed women as equal fishing competitors, a significant part of his ideology that so many critics have conveniently avoided. Hemingway held Helen Lerner, a diminutive woman who was a fierce, strong, and skilled big-game angler, in the highest regard, and the 1930s pictures of him shaking hands on the dock with sportswomen such as Chisie Farrington (Kip's wife) mirror those of him congratulating male anglers for similar prize catches. Hemingway's progressive remarks were published at a time when the larger culture would not have viewed these female anglers in such an egalitarian manner, and Hemingway would have been under no pressure at all to be politically correct in his public attitudes about the pioneering women of the sport. I have located enough evidence to satisfy my conclusion that he truly believed women were just as capable of landing record-breaking fish as he was.

Furthermore, this established view was not one that was necessarily shared by the fraternity of male fishermen who were Hemingway's contemporaries. Kelly writes Tommy Gifford was among the sportsmen (including Hemingway) who "believed that women were fully capable of landing even the biggest of fish" (31). Kelly tells the story of an argument between Farrington and Gifford, writing that Farrington "confidently made the statement that a woman simply could not handle a powerful fish such as a bluefin tuna" (36). Kelly then describes the lengths to which Gifford went in order to prove

Helen Lerner congratulates Hemingway for his catch of this 542-pound blue marlin in Bimini in 1936. Mike Lerner is pictured on the left.

Farrington wrong, including serving as the fishing guide for Helen Lerner as she boated 11 bluefin tuna and helping another female angler boat a bluefin in excess of 400 pounds (37). By demonstrating his belief in women as equal competitors, Hemingway was not only way

Hemingway and Chisie Farrington (wife of Kip Farrington) inspect a 345-pound Bimini blue marlin in June 1936.

ahead of the curve of the culture itself (remember the World War era when America was struggling with the concept of women going into the workforce in the absence of the men who were at war?), he was willing to declare his view even among the most respected sportsmen of his day, many of whom likely disagreed with his position.

What we have in Hemingway's documented remarks about conservation and women as equal sportsmen is ample evidence to support a counternarrative to the kind of bitter criticism that has been allowed to dominate this field largely unchallenged. Any critic who wants to open the can of worms about Hemingway's perceived misogyny or brutality must be willing to dump out and examine the *whole can* of worms. The evidence I have presented here does not necessarily override or completely negate what are some fair criticisms of the Hemingway biography, his sometimes problematic representation of female characters, and remarks he made about women in other contexts. My argument about the laudable characteristics of Hemingway's perception of the competence of women anglers is challenged with evidence such as a March 1936 letter Hemingway sent to Lerner, in which the author wrote, "Between you and me I think that any sporting organization dominated by a woman, no matter how fine and noble that woman, is a pain in the ass to belong to and I would like to resign as soon as possible. The women I admire in sport fishing are your wife Mrs. Lerner and my wife Mrs. Hemingway and when we are hooked into a fish we don't want any advice from any of them" (McIver 124). One's thinking about this issue cannot be confined to a dichotomy, either A) Hemingway was a chauvinist pig or B) Hemingway was a crusader for women's rights. The answer is C) Hemingway was a human being born almost 120 years ago, and his sometimes contradictory worldview is complicated. To fully understand the challenges faced by women in any given time period, one must simultaneously understand the challenges faced by the men of the same generation. It was not an easy thing to be a woman or a man in those bewildering first decades of the 20th century, and as readers looking back at them from a new century, we need to take a deep breath, cut them some slack, and stop trying to categorize them through the lens of our very different perception.

Helen Lerner (far right), who was a fixture on the Bimini docks, is photographed with a blue marlin.

Rules and Equity

All of the available historical evidence from the time Hemingway began saltwater fishing in Key West through the peak of his involvement with the management of the sport through the emergence of the IGFA reveals his belief in the importance of standards and rules to make big-game fishing (at least as far as records) fair to all. He was, as Rivkin indicates, "also extremely high-minded in his approach to the sporting life. [. . .] [H]e would deliberate with great care as to which element of tackle would create the most meaningful sporting experience" (69). Farrington credits Hemingway as one of the first to discern ethical conundrums in fishing practices and then question them (*Fishing with Hemingway and Glassell* 7). As an additional sign of their commitment to parity, the IGFA officers — even though many of them were the most skilled anglers of their day — agreed to refrain from filing for world-record recognition with their catches. Likewise, the processes they developed for certifying world records were quite rigorous. To claim a world record, McIver notes, "an angler's catch must be properly witnessed, weighed at an official weighing station, and documented. Additionally, the line on which the fish was caught must be tested to see that it does not exceed strength specifications" (127). A good portion of the Hemingway-Lerner correspondence in the 1930s is occupied with their discussions of specifications for tackle, procedures, and processes that would advance the stature of big-game fishing as a gentleman's sport whose participants were willing to yield to a unified code of conduct.

Hemingway's IGFA Hall of Fame Induction

For his contributions to the IGFA as a founding officer and to the sport of big-game fishing as a whole, in 1998 Hemingway was inducted posthumously into the IGFA's Fishing Hall of Fame, receiving the honor of induction with the very first class of 29 members.

Since that first class, 76 other anglers have been inducted ("IGFA Hall of Fame Inductees"). The plaques are currently housed on the first floor of the stunning Dania Beach, Florida, facility in a room with 173 life-size fish replicas hanging from the ceiling. The IGFA building is magnificent, with a giant marlin sculpture leaping out of a fountain at the entrance to the museum. You should visit the IGFA at your earliest convenience and bring a camera.

Hemingway's Hall of Fame induction plaque at the IGFA.

Big Changes for the IGFA

The IGFA today is still a thriving organization with a healthy membership worldwide, a success that is a true testament to the dedication and forward thinking of its early leadership. The annual membership rates are very reasonable and the benefits really are extraordinary in comparison to the cost. Unfortunately, in 2015 officials announced

The IGFA Hall of Fame on the first floor of the Dania Beach headquarters.

the IGFA Museum and Hall of Fame would be moving to Spring-field, Missouri, to be part of the new Johnny Morris Wonders of Wildlife National Museum and Aquarium, which will be built beside the flagship Bass Pro Shops Outdoor World. The IGFA E. K. Har-ry Library of Fishes, which contains the most comprehensive set of fishing archives in the world, is staying at the Dania Beach facility along with the IGFA headquarters and staff. The fish replicas in the

Hall of Fame room will remain as well. The reason for the move, as one might expect, is money. The Florida location was not drawing as many visitors as officials had hoped, and the new complex in Missouri (opening in 2016) is expected to attract bigger crowds of tourists.

For a very amateur fisherwoman and a Hemingway scholar, my visit to the Dania Beach headquarters in 2016 was like a dream. The rare books that would normally require interlibrary loans from academic libraries are all there just waiting for the curious reader. A whole room is dedicated to storage of the Mike Lerner photographs. It would be possible to spend weeks in that room alone perusing the images of his brilliant life. Surprising relics that will take your breath away seem to be tucked in every corner, like the iconic Cat Cay Tuna Tournament trophy. Dozens of filing cabinets are stuffed with photographic evidence of the most superb adventures of the best anglers the world has ever known. Only having one day to explore was simultaneously blissful and torturous, but I could have spent a year there and left feeling like there was more to be covered. The library also

The famous Cat Cay Tuna Tournament trophy in the IGFA library.

contains a Hemingway Reading Room, which was donated by Mina Hemingway, Patrick Hemingway's daughter. Located on the second floor of the IGFA facility, the Hemingway Reading Room is the ideal place to peruse a stack of amazing archives retrieved from the library's astonishing collection.

The IGFA stands today as a physical reminder of all that Hemingway meant to the emergence of the sport of big-game fishing and what his legacy still represents for present-day anglers. In a world where fishing technology is changing so rapidly, it is a true pleasure to step back in time in the IGFA archives and see how the pioneers of the sport managed such remarkable catches with archaic tackle that would baffle the young-gun anglers who are now accustomed to the gadgets and gizmos that take so much of the sporting nature of fishing out of the equation. Judging by the letters that passed between Lerner and Hemingway, my guess is that they would both be disgusted by the idea of depth finders and underwater angling cameras that actually show the fish swimming near your boat. In their day, you *learned* your fishing grounds, and as you gained skill, you became attuned to the signs Mother Nature gave you that the big fish were nearby. Considering what 1930s big-game fishermen had to work with, what they had to know, and what they were required to endure to land their world records, I argue no generation of fishermen will ever be as great as Hemingway and his fishing buddies during those enchanted Bimini summers. We need the IGFA to perpetuate the vital work these remarkable fishermen started and to guide the sport in this ever-changing world.

By the time the middle of May rolls around, the giant bluefin
tuna [...] start racing through. You can mark the calendar
by their arrival every year, for they are never off schedule. The
grand procession, probably the greatest in fishdom, is led by
the 300-pounders [...] until the trailers, weighing seven
hundred pounds and more, come through late in June. It is
my belief that a tuna passing Bimini on Monday could attend
church off New Jersey the following Sunday.

— Kip Farrington, *Atlantic Game Fishing*

V
The Great Bimini Mystery:
Did Hemingway Return?

THE PREVIOUS FOUR CHAPTERS solidify Heming-
way's love for Bimini and his enthusiasm for its sporting life.
Every published scholar who has ever written on the topic of
Hemingway's summers in Bimini unequivocally asserts that he never
returned to the island after 1937. This chapter will explore the factors
(some factual and some speculative) that took him away from Bimini
and the many reasons he had to return. Interestingly, the influences
that would have pulled him toward the island were just as numerous
and compelling as those drawing him away. Also fascinating is reasonable interview evidence I gathered suggesting Hemingway may
have returned to the island in the late 1950s. While no proof from
the known correspondence exists to substantiate these claims, the
evidence I uncovered is worth a look, especially considering sizeable
gaps in the late 1950s Hemingway chronology that at least make
these visits a viable possibility.

The Critical Consensus

The last letter placing Hemingway in Bimini was to Waldo Peirce on July 27, 1937. Hemingway left Bimini for his final *Pilar* voyage away from the island on August 2 of that year. Hilary Hemingway doubts the author ever came back after that departure. "If true, there would be press and photos of such an event," she says. "I mean, look at the

Hemingway holds a fishing rod in Bimini in the 1930s.

press clippings from his trip to Spain in 1959. Every day of [his] life after he won the Nobel in '54 is documented — either by press clippings or Ernest's own letters. If he went back, everyone would know it." Leicester Hemingway agreed that his brother never returned, telling Ashley Saunders, "I think something was eating him why he didn't come back. He had many chances to return" (*Volume 1*, 145). Sir Michael Checkley, the Director of the Bimini Museum, concurs. While he suggests the author did not come back, "other family members did continue to visit," he says, "including his brother Leicester and [Ernest Hemingway's] sons John and Gregory. [. . .] Gregory returned often up until a few years before his death, [attending] parts of the 2000 International Hemingway Conference held here."

My initial thought when presented with the reports of Hemingway returning to Bimini was that maybe the islanders had confused Leicester, who was known to look a lot like his brother, with Ernest. When asked directly if this confusion was possible, Hilary Hemingway says with certainty, "It wasn't my father. Dad's life during the 1950s decade was spent working for the U.S. Embassy in Bogotá, Colombia, then in Maryland where he divorced his first wife Patsy, then in NYC in 1955 where he met and married my mother Doris." They lived in New York until the 1960s, when they moved to Miami.

The Bahamas Trip: June 1949

Scholars know for sure that Hemingway returned to the Bahamas in June 1949. The John F. Kennedy Library in Boston houses what exists of Hemingway's boat logs, and the *Pilar* journal from 1945–1949 includes an entry entitled "Log of Bahama Trip" dated June 1949. Carlos Baker's *Ernest Hemingway: A Life Story* says the 1949 excursion was a 10-day affair that included fishing in "Cay Sal, the Anguillas, and the Bahama Banks" (590). The log documents the trip participants: General C. T. Lanham, Raymundo Franchetti, Gregory Hemingway, Gregorio Fuentes, someone named Santiago, and Ernest Hemingway. The members of the fishing party differ in Chamberlin's entry for the Bahamas trip, as he includes "Ginger and Tom (Key West friends of the Bruces, Nanuk (nickname for Mary?), Betty, and Toby Bruce" (274). Baker provides yet another roster, claiming Mayito Menocal, Elicio Arguelles, and Patrick Hemingway were along (590). It is possible the group went to port to allow new friends to join the flotilla. Baker contended the fishing was "phenomenal," as they returned from the trip with nearly 2,000 pounds of fish on ice (591).

Reynolds paints a much different picture of the trip's success, suggesting that the weather was too rough to do any fishing, Gregorio Fuentes was ill, and Gregory Hemingway's appendix required medical attention (202). Regardless of the inconsistencies in the literature about the particulars of this voyage, these sources provide the only hard evidence that Hemingway was fishing in the Bahamas again after 1937. It is important to note the fishing grounds for this trip were technically in the Bahamas, but the destinations for this particular trip were very far away from Bimini. Boating back up to the island from those locations would have been quite a journey in the *Pilar*.

The Spanish Civil War

The first compelling reason critics have cited as evidence of Hemingway not returning to the island is his preoccupation with the Spanish Civil War, which ran from 1936 to 1939. Hemingway had more than just a passing interest in the conflict. In late 1936, he received a request to cover the war and officially signed a contract with the North American Newspaper Alliance in early 1937. John Patrick Hemingway reported in 2013 that "after covering the fall of Madrid to the Fascists [Ernest] moved to Cuba," never to return to Bimini. Watson encapsulates precisely how the Spanish conflict shattered Hemingway's tropical Eden. Once Hemingway returned from Spain, "he headed straight for Bimini, hoping, no doubt, for some respite from the physical and emotional demands that the war had put upon him" (141). His recess in Bimini that summer did not come to pass, as he was continually pulled away by obligations related to the war. He traveled with Joris Ivens, a documentary producer who convinced the author to help with the film *The Spanish Earth*, to New York in early June. Hemingway later tried to get back in his Bimini groove, but he was called again to New York in June to complete his narration for the project. Watson says that afterward, Hemingway returned to Bimini again to resume his leisure, but his trip only lasted a few days before he was drawn away once more to promote the film (141). Roy Bosche's Hemingway "Reminiscence" in Lawrence's *Prowling Papa's Waters* sheds even more light on the diversion the Spanish Civil War was for the author: "His fishing routine was different during this period [1937] because there were a lot of interruptions" and the war weighed heavily on him (144). Bosche remembers 1937 was different because the author "hadn't assembled his usual Cuban crew. I guess it was because he was pretty sure this trip would be brief" (144). Bimini fishing in 1937 was stellar, making Hemingway's decision to forgo another season on the sea even more compelling. By then, he was famous enough in Bimini for the other fishermen to wonder where he was, prompting Erl Roman in a 1938 article for *Motor Boating* magazine to announce Hemingway's absence from the island was due to the war (19–20).

Hemingway's correspondence also chronicles the author's adventures during the Spanish struggle. From safari on February 3, 1937, Helen Lerner wrote to Pauline and Ernest to tell them the Lerners were following coverage of the author's wartime exploits on their camp radio. In a letter to Lerner on March 4, 1937, Hemingway announced his impending Spanish trip but promised to come back to Bimini in May. Hemingway assured Lerner he was "holding the thought of being there" as a touchstone to get him through the difficult weeks ahead. While acknowledging Lerner might think the trip was "sort of goofy," it was necessary in the author's view to reveal to the world the face of war so that hopefully his sons would never have to be on the front lines. It must have been surreal — and quite troubling — to move between the utopic world of Bimini and the ravaged war zone of Spain. That he was willing to leave paradise (and the comforts of his home and young family) to risk death in order to make a difference with his writing says a great deal about his constitution. In contrast, it is also revealing that Hemingway was accompanied in Spain and on the other work and promotional trips to New York and Washington, D.C., by Martha Gellhorn. Their budding relationship thousands of miles away from Hemingway's marital and family obligations precipitated the many changes that would come upon his return to the States.

Marital Angst, a New Wife, and an International Move

The years of the Spanish Civil War and the year after its conclusion were tumultuous ones for Hemingway. In 1939, he headed to Cuba. The extramarital relationship with Gellhorn was in full swing as the marriage to Pauline was deteriorating. In 1940, Hemingway finally divorced Pauline, and he and Martha moved in at the Finca Vigía, first renting the home and then buying it in December of that year. Hilary Hemingway argues the timing of the relationship with Martha was one of the main reasons the author pulled away from Bimini:

> Yes, he got super busy with Spain, but he was also focused on changing wives. I suspect that Martha did not want Ernest to hang out with his old Bimini sportsman gang. She did not like them any more than she liked his Crook Factory guys. After their affair was off and running, Martha did not visit any places where [he] had lived with his first two wives. Well, the war-torn Spain that Martha was in clearly is not the Fiesta [of San Fermìn] that Pauline enjoyed. So yes, Ernest did keep busy by writing about the Spanish Civil War

(North American Newspaper Dispatches, *The Spanish Earth* documentary, the writing of *For Whom Bell Tolls* and *The Fifth Column*.) But it's not as simple as he was only writing and hadn't time to fish. Ernest enjoyed being with and traveling with Martha. It was Martha who started [his] summers in Sun Valley. This meant Ernest would miss the summer's billfish run off Bimini and Havana. I think Martha helped Ernest drift away from the Bimini sportsmen. I mean, Ernest made new friends pretty easy — made quite a few during the Spanish Civil War.

The drastic life changes that characterized Hemingway's life in these years in and of themselves would have been sufficient reason to delay a Bimini return. However, Hilary Hemingway's insight about Martha's influence on his travel habits is indeed fascinating.

Career Intervention

As one would expect, Hemingway's correspondence throughout his life refers to his level of professional productivity and how he felt about the progression of his ongoing projects. In 1935, Hemingway was forced to decline a fabulous offer from Mike Lerner to go on African safari. The author wrote on August 18 of that year that he had hunted and fished the majority of the months in the past two years and that it was time to "buckle down now and work at something [. . .] for a while." Similarly, in 1938 after the Lerners offered Hemingway the vacant Anchorage, he declined but reiterated he would rather be in Bimini than anywhere else if only he did not "have to stick to this damned work" (Outgoing Correspondence, July 18, 1938, JFK). The years after the Bimini summers became a pressure-filled time in Hemingway's career as he felt the squeeze to produce a masterpiece. On April 4, 1939, Hemingway mailed fisherman Tommy Shevlin an apology letter for backing out of participating on his team in a fishing tournament. The professional pickle he cited reveals an intriguing snapshot of what Hemingway was feeling about his work at the time. He explained that a short story he intended to write had turned into a novel — what would eventually become *The Old Man and the Sea*. After describing all of his interruptions in Key West, he shared with Shevlin his fear of losing his grasp on the project because of his inability to focus on it. The pressure he felt to produce was in plain sight: he had to get this one right. Hemingway summed up his

Mike Lerner salutes Hemingway on an impressive Bimini catch.
Carlos Gutiérrez stands to the far right.

quandary to Shevlin succinctly: he could not travel as a "sportsman and write a novel" concurrently. Unlike many other people, Hemingway felt confident Shevlin would understand his inability to "jump in and out" of his work. While he had managed to produce magazine articles and other short pieces and edit the proofs of larger works, Hemingway needed adequate space in his schedule to crank out the novel he so desperately needed. With no permanent home in Bimini, perhaps he realized he could not establish an effective writing routine there.

The Big Fish Have Gone?

By the time the late 1930s rolled around, the fishing landscape in Bimini had certainly begun to change. Watson notes the negative effects commercial fishing had on the island after 1937 (141). A perusal of the Mike Lerner–Hemingway Bimini photo archives at the IGFA certainly makes one wonder how many fish these men actually left in the ocean. Bimini now had worldwide notoriety for its fishing treasures, so the number of anglers who descended upon the tiny island for the season each year had risen exponentially as well. In the July 18, 1938, letter Hemingway sent Lerner from Key West, the author pondered the possibility that the number of mammoth fish were finite in any given area and that the biggest ones in places like Bimini and New Zealand may have already been bagged. Clarifying he does not believe there are no more *granders* to be had, he suggested the quantity of "over-size [. . .] big old fish" would likely decline. The reader senses his hunch that perhaps the Bimini peak has already occurred.

A Conquered Fishing Ground?

Because Hemingway waited so long to come over to Bimini in the first place, even after hearing about its world-class fishing grounds, and because he desired proficiency with his own boat and angling skills before he came, it is conceivable he felt he had conquered Bimini as an angler, especially after landing the first unmutilated tuna there. After being so very involved in the formative years of the sport of big-game fishing, it really is startling how quickly Hemingway pulled back and began to focus on other things. Perhaps he felt he had really become one of the best and was ready to move on to a new arena of challenge. Maybe the fact that he could not hold any world records because of his position as a vice president with the IGFA made him lose his competitive fire. His notoriety on the island could have also paralyzed his ability to come into town for pure relaxation. It is conceivable as well that he recognized Bimini for the utopia that it was and understood that a paradise so perfect was destined for corruption. Like a new favorite food consumed to excess that quickly loses its flavor, maybe Hemingway extracted everything he felt the island had to offer. Bimini for him could have been a fire that burned too hot and fast to sustain itself.

Hemingway's Obsession Cools?

The ongoing Hemingway letters project by the Hemingway Foundation and Hemingway Society is so vital to the field because these documents reveal what was occupying Hemingway's mind and time outside of his published writing. You can see, for instance, how a new woman in his life, like Gellhorn in the 1930s or Mary Welsh in the 1940s, consumed his thinking. During those courting and honeymoon phases, his letters became very sappy, and he really stopped writing to anyone else for a time. The lucky reader afforded the chance to examine the entire outgoing correspondence clearly sees the singular theme of the letters from the early and middle years of the 1930s: fishing. It is appropriate to call Hemingway's interest an obsession. As Ott points out, the "height of the marlin season runs from late April to August, and from 1932 to 1937, Hemingway arranged his life to spend those months on the Gulf Stream" (7). The fishing letters are copious, detailed, thoughtful, and lengthy, providing the perfect illustration of the author's complete concentration on learning. Once the reader gets into 1937 and especially into 1938 and beyond, it is evident that fishing discussions and descriptions do not take up near-ly as much space in Hemingway's letters as they did in previous years.

This is not to suggest that he lost his passion for fishing. In February of 1937, for instance, he added upgrades to the *Pilar* such as better outriggers and a new helm control (Chamberlin 178). He continued to fish well and often for many years in Cuba, and writing about the ocean occupied his creative world after the Bimini sum-mers with works such as *Islands in the Stream* and *The Old Man and the Sea*. "Clearly, Ernest never could have written a book like *The Old Man and the Sea*," Hilary Hemingway says, "if he had fallen out of love with fishing. I think that is why he presented Santiago's story as pure, a fight between man and fish. Not with rod and reel. Not with a motor and teasers, but with a sail and oars. No tricks or gimmicks, fishing simply as man has done for thousands of years." The most objective statement to be made about this issue, I think, is that his zeal was dampened just a bit.

Hilary Hemingway also adds to the discussion the possibility that her uncle was disenchanted with what sport fishing was becom-ing in those years after the formation of the IGFA. "He [. . .] was falling out of love with the rich boys who were doing all the big-game fishing," she contends. Carlos Baker argued that by 1936, the author "was beginning to fear that his widening acquaintance among the rich might harm his integrity as a writer" (366). Therefore, both personal irritation and discomfort with the wealthy and a fear of their impact on his craft could have influenced his decision to stay away from Bimini, where the especially wealthy anglers seemed to out-number the conch shells.

Questioning Loyalties

The next chapter will deal exclusively with the large plot of Bimini land Hemingway came to own with Mike Lerner's assistance. Embedded within this transaction is the possibility that Hemingway questioned his friend's motivation. Hilary Hemingway's opinion is that "Ernest may have felt that the reason Lerner gave the land to him in the first place was because Ernest was able to give ink to the promotion of big-game fishing in Bimini. Nobody likes being used, but as Ernest got more famous, he probably started to question the loyalties of everyone around him." By the last years of his life when his fame was at a crescendo and his increasing mental illness and paranoia came into play, he certainly had to be questioning the motives of all who were in his circle. With fame naturally comes the multitude of beggars

Carlos Gutiérrez, Captain Fred Lister, Mike Lerner, Ernest Hemingway, and Julio Sanchez display their rods and their fishing prizes in Bimini in 1935.

and manipulators jockeying for their piece of someone else's pie. In his final years, he was, according to Hilary Hemingway, "[m]arried to Mary, but wanting Adriana [Ivancich]." Then he lost "his self-confidence in 1950 with his first big, bad book review of *Across the River and into the Trees*." After the *New York Times* printed he was "all but washed up," she explains, Hemingway was "on the defensive, both in print and in life. But then everything changes two years later with the success of *The Old Man and the Sea*. Ernest goes from self-loathing to self-importance. And as the book wins the various awards, he starts to question the loyalties of all who surround him. Do they love me, or my fame? Are they trying to use me? It happens with celebrity." I am sure there were many people in Hemingway's life who remained there merely for their own benefit. From my perspective, looking back at these letters and this history, it does not appear that Lerner's motives were anything but true. My viewpoint, however, does not matter; Hemingway's appraisal of the relationship at the time may have been enough to make him suspicious of the Bimini crowd.

Bimini Was Still Calling

Despite the catalog of very reasonable explanations that would account for Hemingway's reluctance to return to Bimini after 1937, the island still had the potential to hold a great deal of allure for the author. A letter to Max Perkins in July 1935 encapsulated the island's attraction perfectly: "Good fishing, wonderful swimming, nice people – fine climate." He would prefer to stay, he told Perkins, but he feared for the *Pilar* during the hurricane months. It is hard to imagine that his intense passion for the island ever waned. When considering whether or not to travel, the love one has for a place will almost always trump any other reason to deter a trip. Even though I can think of 1,000 valid and mature reasons I should not go to Key West, the simple fact that *I want to* overrules them all year after year. It just seems odd Hemingway could be so energized about Bimini during those three summers and *never* go back. Hemingway's immense love for the island was evident as late the March 4, 1937, letter to Lerner. He confided he was ready to put the Spanish Civil War behind him and focus instead on the sight of the "wonderful beach" in Bimini where he could "feel the old Gulf Stream water" on his toes before embarking on a day of fishing. The Bimini years really could be counted among the best of the author's life. As the distance from those 1930s summers grew longer, it is evident in the letters from both Hemingway and Lerner that their fondness for those golden memories intensified. It is certainly tenable Hemingway would have wanted to revisit the island if only for a short time to rekindle those great memories and visit a very dear old friend.

Lerner Hospitality

The Lerners were unbelievably generous to the Hemingways with their hospitality. Even though the author never built a home on the island, the Lerner-Hemingway correspondence makes it abundantly clear that he always had a lovely place to stay on the island with hosts who repeatedly begged him to visit in their letters. On May 19, 1936, for instance, Helen Lerner invited the Hemingways to the Anchorage, which she was taking great care to prepare for them ahead of their arrival, even pre-ordering supplies so they would be completely comfortable as soon as they got there. Similarly, in a letter from Mike Lerner on June 5, 1936, at a time when Hemingway and Pauline were at the Anchorage, he reminded them that they were to treat themselves as if they were at their own home when they were there. Multiple letters throughout the late 1930s from the Lerners encourage Hemingway to use the house any way he pleased, even while the Lerners are away from the island. This standing invitation essentially gave Hemingway his own fabulous private house in Bimini rent-free and often for months at a time. For a few full seasons in the late 1930s, the Lerners were never in Bimini. This correspondence shows them to be exceptionally gracious hosts, and they often offered the services of their own staff even on Hemingway family visits when the Lerners were not in residence.

Mike Lerner's generosity with Hemingway extended beyond the land deal that essentially gave Hemingway the Bimini property and past Helen and Mike's overwhelming magnanimity with the Anchorage and their staff. Multiple letters that passed between Hemingway and Lerner in the late 1930s indicate Lerner acted as Hemingway's pro bono financial advisor in many matters. Lerner often made investments for the author using his own personal funds (including stock purchases and trades and annuity investments) and then transferred the profits (some of which were substantial) afterward, apparently sometimes even without Hemingway's prior knowledge. In a letter of December 15, 1935, from Hemingway to Lerner, he referenced a stock trade that netted him more than $1,000 over a weekend. This event, Hemingway joked, was the antithesis of all he knew of "the stock market and the human race." One letter even suggested Lerner planned to give the Hemingway children stock in his company. The fabulous wealth of the Lerners allowed them to travel and live on a completely different level than the Hemingways, but the Lerner munificence was extended to the author and his family so many times. Complicating this scenario, however, could have been Hemingway's previously discussed suspicion about incredibly wealthy people. Lerner's generosity could have been viewed by Hemingway with wariness. Considering Hemingway's relatively humble upbringing, it had to be quite peculiar to receive unexpected checks in the mail from what might have felt like a benefactor, all the while knowing he could never possibly reciprocate the generosity. Such actions (no matter how well-intentioned) could have made Hemingway uncomfortable and possibly even caused hard feelings. Two other interpersonal situations between Hemingway and Lerner that may have created a strained friendship will be discussed in the next chapter as well.

As a literary celebrity, Hemingway is famous for the illustrious company he kept. Most great writers are known to be excellent observers of human behavior and interaction, and the conversation of good company allows them to keep their creative juices fresh. Among the who's who of actors, writers, journalists, editors, and sportsmen who could be counted as close Hemingway friends (many of whom were in Bimini in those amazing years), Mike Lerner was probably the most fascinating, especially considering Lerner and Hemingway's shared interest in fishing and hunting.

So, Did Hemingway Come Back?

Even though it is established in the literature that Hemingway did not return to the island after the summer of 1937, and I have catalogued many convincing reasons that Bimini was no longer a perfect fit, I am still not satisfied that he never went back to the island to visit. Any long-term fishing he did in Bimini in those later years would have certainly been documented by now. A short visit (or a series of quick trips) cannot be definitively ruled out, however. Considering the tremendous allure of the island for Hemingway and the fact that he had strong personal connections to Bimini, a breathtaking plot of land at his disposal, and a boat for manageable transport from his existing homes in Key West and Cuba, I will not back away from the possibility that he *might* have visited until every single day of his life after 1937 is credibly accounted for. In the years after 1937, he traveled all over the globe. As such, I would find it counterintuitive if he did not go back at least once in light of Bimini's proximity.

I embarked upon my research at the John F. Kennedy Library in Boston and the International Game Fish Association in Dania Beach, Florida, with a mind open to the idea that Hemingway may actually have returned to the island at some point or even on multiple occasions. Excluding the boat log evidence from 1949 and the correspondence proving he was in the Bahamas in that year, there is no existing archival evidence placing Hemingway on the island again after 1937. Be that as it may, it is impossible for every detail of even a very famous person's life to be recorded by historians and archivists.

On my first full day on the island in January 2016, I had the pleasure of interviewing Thomas Saunders in his lovely front yard, which is filled with the seashells, intricate crafts, and jewelry he sells. He lives at the corner of Saunders Street and the King's Highway on the property between the Anchorage and Hemingway's lot. Saunders, born in 1939, was not alive when Hemingway visited in 1935–37, though he is certainly well-versed in the island's Hemingway lore, as are most Biminites of his generation. When asked if he knew of anything that happened with Hemingway on the island that would make him not want to return after 1937, he responded by saying, "No, I didn't know what happened then. When he did come back, I was pretty young. When he was here in the 1930s, I wasn't even born yet. I didn't really even see him until 1957." Saunders's mention of Hemingway returning in 1957 caught my attention, so I double-checked the date with him to confirm: "So he was here in 1957?" Saunders said without hesitation, "He was here in 1957." When I asked what Hemingway was doing on the island, he pointed toward the Anchorage and said, "He was over here at Lerner's. He visited over there, but he didn't go out much." Saunders indicated Hemingway was there for "a couple of days" — just one or two. I asked again just to make sure

Ansil Saunders sits outside his boat shop in Bailey Town. He is well known for his craftsmanship and his dedication to the art of boat building.

Saunders was not confused: "So you are saying 1957 — not 1937 — because you would have been old enough to remember it." He replied, "Yes. As far as I know, he didn't ever fish. You know, what happens here on the island, I don't care if you are a star or whatever — people [don't] pay too much attention to you, you know like that. The natives see you a couple of times, and they just view you as one of the people here."

Another Saunders family member, Ansil, was also interviewed a few days later about the matter of Hemingway returning to the island in the 1950s. A world-famous bonefisherman and guide, Ansil is also known for his boat-crafting skill. Born in 1932, he was probably old enough to remember Hemingway in the 1930s. Ansil confirmed Hemingway did come back to Bimini in the 1950s, but he says it was "not often." He remembers "maybe three times," and during those brief visits, Hemingway "wasn't talking to people." He claims the author "stayed in Lerner's yard at the cottage. Lerner didn't have him in the big house. [He stayed] in the little cottage in Lerner's yard — near Weech's dock and Brown's dock." He said the cottage is a "wash house" now. When Hemingway returned for those brief trips, Ansil asserted Hemingway was "still doing mischief" on the island like he did in the 1930s.

Cleveland Francis, another Bimini native I met on Saunders Street, also asserts Hemingway was back on the island in 1957. Born in 1945, Francis would have been old enough to remember any 1950s visits, and when asked if Hemingway came to Bimini that year, he said, "Oh yeah. That's right." Francis claims Hemingway was on the island to fish, though he did not bring the *Pilar* with him. Instead, he says the author stayed with the Lerners and went out on their boat a few times, and they caught some wahoo. Francis says he remembers because he helped Hemingway clean the fish afterward. Other islanders who were asked the same questions about Hemingway's return agree he did come back, though they are vague about the years and generally seem to agree on the late 1950s as the time period. These natives also allege he came to the island in those later years to be alone and was not out and about in a visible way on the island. One interview subject said Hemingway would leave after a few days once it became known on the island that he was there. If he was in Bimini in the late 1950s, he apparently did not want any publicity.

Several significant gaps in the Hemingway timeline exist that at least open the possibility that these natives are right. These blocks are much easier to identify now that Chamberlin's comprehensive *Hemingway Log* is available. Multiple open times exist between 1955 and 1960 in which Hemingway could have potentially traveled to an undocumented place. The chart on the next page outlines those significant blocks of time chronologically.

The chart demonstrates the sizable chunks of time available to Hemingway for travel to Bimini under the radar. For a number of reasons, 1957 seems very plausible to me. First, Hemingway had the time to go as it appears February through September of that year were open. Secondly, in August of 1957, Hemingway's dog was shot and killed by the Cuban police at the Finca Vigía. The Cuban Revolution was in full swing by that time, making the Hemingways' lives there uncomfortable, so it would make sense that he could have wanted to take a trip to get away and to do so unnoticed.

The major complication to my theory about the late 1950s is the state of Hemingway's health during those years. A picture of Hemingway with several fish in 1954 Cuba in Kelly's *Florida's Fishing Legends and Pioneers* proves he was still out and about on the *Pilar*, though he was clearly aged by that time. He was bedridden with illness from late 1955 to early 1956 but was stable enough to travel to Peru for movie filming. According to Farrington, the Peruvian trek for *The Old Man and the Sea* movie was the only example of the author fishing outside of Florida, Cuba, or the Bahamas, but the trip was necessary because a fish of the size they needed for the film

Hemingway Travel: 1955–1960

Ernest and Mary spent the entire year of 1955 in Cuba except for a Key West trip from July 3 to 7.

By November 1955, Hemingway was bedridden with illness and remained there until January 1956.

In April to May 1956, Hemingway was well enough to participate in the filming of *The Old Man and the Sea* movie in Peru.

On May 23, 1956, the Hemingways were back in Cuba.

The next trip was in the middle of August to New York to catch a steamer for Europe. On September 1, they boarded the *Ile de France*, and they remained in Europe through January 23, 1957, before taking the same ship home. Ernest stayed on the vessel after the New York stop to travel in the Caribbean.

By February 14, both Hemingways were in Cuba.

Next was Hemingway's trip to New York in September 1957. He then traveled to Washington, D.C., before coming back to Cuba in October.

Aside from a trip in October 1957 to visit Gregory at the Miami Medical Center, Hemingway was working in Cuba for the remainder of the year.

It is not until September 30, 1958, that he and Mary left for Idaho. They returned to Cuba on March 29, 1959.

On April 22, 1959, they were off to New York, Spain, and then France.

They were back in the United States by October 1959, with Hemingway in residence in Havana on November 4.

On November 11, he went to Key West before returning to Idaho.

The Hemingways came back to Cuba for the last time on January 17, 1960.

(Chamberlin 296–300, 302, 304–316, 318)

could only be captured in Peru (*Fishing with Hemingway and Glassell* 20). A letter from Mary Hemingway to Bill Seward on August 22, 1958, painted a very grim picture of the author's declining health, as she claimed he had been "enslaved" by a "thing" for a year or so and had not really left his Cuban house very much. Reading the accounts of his final spiral toward suicide, including A. E. Hotchner's *Heming-*

way in Love: His Own Story, is heartbreaking. Hotchner describes his failed attempts to divert Hemingway's attention from his ailments by planning trips to the fishing locations of the author's past (4–5). In light of the magnitude of the mental struggles he was facing and his hospitalizations and treatments, fishing was probably very far from his mind. There is no evidence placing Hemingway on the *Pilar* after May 19, 1960, according to Hendrickson's exhaustive research about the boat (606).

So, the question of Hemingway's return to Bimini is still open for debate. Thomas Saunders's position on this issue is particularly credible because he worked for the Lerners — both at the Lerner Marine Laboratory and at their home. Additionally, Thomas's house is right next door to the Anchorage. My perception of the issue may be skewed because I want so much to believe Hemingway returned. Even if I do not have hard evidence to prove my case about a 1950s Bimini visit by Hemingway, in my imagination at least he did return for one last look at the Gulf Stream from that incredible tropical vista on the King's Highway.

[T]he great, deep blue river, three quarters of a mile to a mile
deep and sixty to eighty miles across [...] has, when the
river is right, the finest fishing I have ever known.

— Hemingway, "The Great Blue River," *Holiday* July 1949

VI
The King's Highway Property Question Unraveled

THE MAJORITY of this text has focused on Bimini's relationship to Hemingway, the IGFA, and the birth of sport fishing on a macro level. This chapter will shift gears to focus in a microscopic way on the single element of the Hemingway-Bimini story that has puzzled me the most. Multiple scholarly sources mention the Alice Town land on the King's Highway that Michael Lerner either gave or sold Hemingway to entice him to build and take up permanent residence. The land is located on the south side of North Bimini. From the Queen's Highway, take Saunders Street to connect with the King's Highway. At the top of the hill after you pass the Dolphin House, the tract of land is on the right. While Hemingway owned the parcel, there was no structure built on the property. The house that was eventually constructed was for sale at the time of this writing with an asking price of $1.8 million, and it enjoys a permanently unobstructed view of the most beautiful beach I have ever seen. The sapphire waters of the Gulf Stream unfold like a beautiful blue ribbon on the horizon and can be seen from the home's front yard. It is really impossible to conceive of a more gorgeous place to build a home. Even more enticing is that the white sand beach — dotted each morning with the most perfect conch shells — is utterly deserted. Hemingway would have been able to enjoy interrupted privacy there. The correspondence between Hemingway and Lerner housed at the John F. Kennedy Library is inconsistent on the name of the man who owned the parcel before Mike Lerner: either Sailing Baruch (Incoming Correspondence, November 19, 1936, October 30, 1943, and June 21, 1950, JFK) or Saling Brooks (Incoming Correspondence, May 22, 1937, JFK). What is clear is that the transaction turned into a problematic arrangement that was not sorted out until after Hemingway's death in 1961.

The view down Saunders Street from the King's Highway. Hemingway's lot is on the left, and Thomas Saunders's house is on the right.

When talking to knowledgeable Bimini natives about the issue of the land, the language about the deal varies from "gave" to "sold," and the same variance is seen in the scholarship about the transaction. Archival research reveals the reason for the confusion. The first letter between Hemingway and Lerner referencing the land comes on December 3, 1935. In it, Hemingway said he enclosed "the check for the tract of land in Bimini," and he expressed sincere gratitude for Lerner's facilitation of the deal. Remember Hemingway and Lerner had only known each other since the spring of that same year, and by December, the author was paying for his share of a permanent slice of the island, a testament to his immediate infatuation with Bimini. It could be argued Hemingway would have never taken action independently of Lerner's help to become a landowner on the island, but the deal transpired nonetheless.

This house now sits on the land Mike Lerner gifted to Hemingway. The home was for sale at the time of publication for $1.8 million, its price due to the property's permanently unobstructed view of Radio Beach. According to Thomas Saunders, Hemingway's widow gave the land to the American Museum of Natural History after his death, and it was later sold.

We know from Lerner's response nine days later that a check for $200 was indeed enclosed. This letter of December 12, 1935, contains the first of many references by Lerner to what would become the laborious process of converting the deed into Hemingway's name. The concept of buying this exquisite piece of property for only $200 makes the transaction seem much more like a gift than a business deal. Just one year later, Lerner notified Hemingway that the land was likely worth $1,500, and even then, Lerner may have been underestimating its value (Incoming Correspondence, April 7, 1936, JFK). We should all be so lucky to have friends as magnanimous as Mike Lerner.

Facing Radio Beach, the property sits adjacent on the right to the house owned by Thomas Saunders. Saunders's parcel was purchased from Lerner in a deal very similar to Hemingway's. Saunders explained in a personal interview, "I bought this land from the Lerners — late 1960," a time when the property would have been much

Thomas Saunders's house sits in between Hemingway's land and the Anchorage. A small church separates Saunders's property and the Lerner land. The Dolphin House can be seen in the background.

more valuable than when the Hemingway transaction took place in 1935. Saunders then built his current house in 1968. It is apparent through these very generous transactions that Lerner was a benevolent man first and foremost. Additionally, he was interested in creating a fishing compound surrounded by the very best neighbors, a fact further corroborated by the correspondence that is to come.

An intriguing development in the ongoing land saga arises in a letter from Hemingway to Lerner on December 15, 1935. In it, the author references a second piece of property that abutted the parcel he had already purchased for $200. The letter suggested Lerner initially refused payment for the second tract but then accepted $25. For a total of $225, Hemingway joked, he had "become a large landholder in the British Dominions." If the first tract of land Hemingway paid $200 for was not a gift, the second plot certainly was. The same letter refers to a stock trade Lerner was facilitating on behalf of the author. Hemingway insisted he would use the profits from the transaction "when we build on Bimini." This proposition is the first written ar-

The steps leading up to the Lerner Anchorage from the Queen's Highway.

chival evidence establishing his intent to construct a home on the island. At the very same moment, correspondence from Lerner to Hemingway indicates the construction of the Anchorage complex was ongoing (Incoming Correspondence, December 20, 1935, JFK). Lerner sent along several photographs to show the author the property's transformation. This letter is the first time the name the Lerners chose for the Anchorage is revealed.

Over the next year, numerous letters between Hemingway and Lerner discuss the matter of the Bimini deed. Apparently, Nassau in those days worked at a snail's pace to approve and transfer legal documents. In the written conversations for the remaining years, what Lerner has to say about the land in general exceeds Hemingway's input on the matter by a very wide margin. Notably, Hemingway wrote to Lerner on March 23, 1936, and actually seemed eager about the deed to the property, asking if "the land titles [are] coming on all right." Granted, it is extraordinarily difficult to accurately appraise emotions in written letters. As well, phone conversations were likely taking place regularly between Hemingway and Lerner at this time. Hemingway may have been giddy about the prospect of building on the land all along. Based on the historical record, however, this March 23rd document represents the only perceived excitement about building Hemingway ever demonstrates in his catalogued letters. What follows are many years of Lerner writing more letters to Hemingway than it appears the author reciprocated and Lerner's tone deteriorating from friendly to very anxious for reasons we will soon explore.

The next wrinkle in the story comes on April 7, 1936, when Lerner reveals to Hemingway he was approached by a man named Mr. Cook who was interested in acquiring land in Bimini for a future home of his own. The parcel that piqued Cook's curiosity adjoined Hemingway's expanded plot running back down the hill to Bimini Harbor. The letter is a bit unclear, but my interpretation is that the land was owned by Lerner when Cook approached him because

Lerner tells Hemingway it was his intent to hold the land in case Hemingway ever built and wanted a harbor-to-sea parcel like Lerner would eventually own on the other side of Saunders Street. None of the correspondence indicates whether Cook bought the land or whether Hemingway took Lerner's offer to expand his Bimini parcel for a third time.

The letters from Lerner for the rest of 1936 and on into 1937 affirm the situation with the transfer of the deed to Hemingway evolved into a hot mess. We know that as of June 1937, Lerner was *still* writing to Hemingway trying to figure out if the Bahamian government had come through with his deed. Action was apparently taken by Lerner on Hemingway's behalf to contact a high-ranking Bahamian official, who assured Lerner the deed would be processed within two months (Incoming Correspondence, June 7, 1937, JFK). There is no more mention of the deed process in future letters between Hemingway and Lerner, so the document was definitely delivered at some point. Later correspondence in which Lerner actually asks for the deed to be returned also substantiates this fact.

Hemingway and Lerner were together in Bimini in the summer of 1937, so they likely talked through the situation with the land and the deed (Incoming Correspondence, July 30, 1937, JFK). The author felt comfortable enough to visit Lerner's home and fish with him that year, so their relationship was probably still on solid footing. The letters passing between Lerner and Hemingway over the next several years do not mention the land or the deed. The Spanish Civil War was raging, and Lerner was aware of Hemingway's involvement in covering it. The reader gets the sense from his writing that Lerner was the kind of man to put business to the side when a friend was facing more pressing matters. If he did have questions or concerns about the deed or the land, I can envision him keeping that uncertainty to himself. Likewise, you will recall from Chapter IV that the Bahamas Marlin and Tuna Club and the IGFA were coming together during these same years, so Lerner and Hemingway were likely in regular contact by telephone, which would have provided ample time for discussions about lingering issues in Bimini.

By 1943, a shift in the correspondence demonstrates Lerner's feelings about Hemingway's Bimini property were changing. Reading the remaining letters and cables exchanged between the two for the next 16 years is uncomfortable. The JFK Collection includes a Western Union telegram from Hemingway to Lerner on June 20, 1943. In a few short words, Hemingway expressed that he "had always hoped" to construct a home on the island but that he would be willing to return the property if that was Lerner's wish. We learn in a later letter that Lerner did ask to have the property back. It is also entirely possible Hemingway at some point started to feel uneasy with the whole arrangement. The next day, Lerner responded with a Western Union message of his own to inform Hemingway he had purchased even more Bimini land on the ocean side. Lerner also expressed his pleasure at the news that Hemingway was going to construct a home on the Bimini land (Incoming Correspondence, June 21, 1943). As the scholar attempting to sort through these details many years removed from when the events took place, I am at the disadvantage of having to speculate. Having just gained even more Bimini property, Lerner did not particularly need the plot of land Hemingway owned. Reading Hemingway's June 20 cable, I hear regret: that he *hoped* to build there but it is just not working out, hence the reason he offers to return the land. It seems to me Lerner's assumption that Hemingway *will build* quite possibly reads more into Hemingway's message than the text supported, especially considering the later correspondence and the fact that Hemingway had allegedly not even been to the island in the six years since the purchase. If he intended to have some kind of permanent presence on the island in the future, it would seem Hemingway would have at least dropped in for a visit occasionally.

On the very next day, another incoming letter from Lerner appears in the Hemingway Collection archive (Incoming Correspondence, June 22, 1943, JFK). The document is fascinating for several reasons. First, Lerner explained he purchased even more land in Bimini, making it clear his intent was to buy as much property around the Anchorage as he could to protect his privacy. Secondly, the land purchase also provided an additional buffer for Hemingway's parcel, which would afford him more seclusion if he built as well. Additionally and perhaps most importantly, Lerner expressed doubt about whether Hemingway even still owned his parcel, bringing up a theme that resonates throughout Lerner's remaining correspondence: *please tell me what is going on with this land. I want you as my Bimini neighbor and no one else.*

As the years progressed, Lerner's doubt and anxiety transitioned into what feels a bit like panic. Hemingway's reluctance to build and then his comparative lack of requital in letter writing gave Lerner cause for concern. On June 30, 1943, Hemingway sent Lerner an apology for not corresponding more often, suggesting that he had been working a great deal. He claimed he would have written more often except that "there is nothing that I know" that might interest Lerner. In this instance, being a scholar with access to other correspondence is helpful, as the archive proves Hemingway did indeed have plenty to write about during this time, as evidenced by the prolific and extended love letters that were pouring into Martha Gellhorn's mailbox. This letter referenced the Bimini deed for the first time in many years, with Hemingway claiming to have it in his possession in Key West. Again, he expressed his willingness to turn the land back over to Lerner. Hemingway told his friend he "would love to build there" but that circumstances (including World War II, among other things) had prevented it. If the theme of Lerner's letters became *please tell me what is going on with this land. I want you as my Bimini neighbor and no one else*, the mantra of Hemingway's responses was *just take back the land if it means that much to you.* Approximately two weeks after Hemingway's letter, Lerner responded on July 13, 1943, insisting he did not want the property back and was content as long as Hemingway kept it in his possession and never sold it to anyone else.

Mike Lerner boating a giant bluefin tuna in Bimini. Erl Roman's caption for the photo explains, "A section of the boat's transom has been removed and the big finster is pulled into the cockpit over a roller that is built into the transom for this purpose."

The Heilner-Lerner Argument

In the fall of 1943, an interesting twist was added to the situation when Van Campen Heilner and Lerner got into quite an argument. Sorting through the dilemma required locating letters at both the John F. Kennedy Library and the American Museum of Natural History Library. On March 17, 1943, Heilner cabled longtime AMNH staffer Francesca LaMonte to ask her to "contact [the] powers that be for official commission for [Hemingway] to fly museum flag on his boat and have credentials for work he is doing for museum in Cuban waters." Heilner expressed the urgency of the request as the expedition was about to commence (Central Archives, 1216, AMNH).

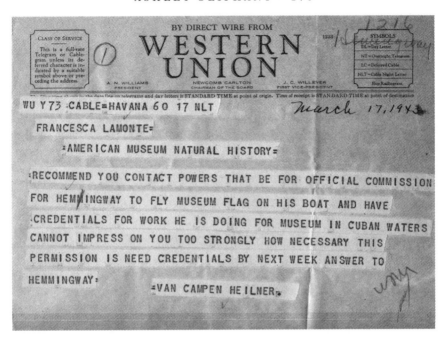

LaMonte informed Hemingway by cable on March 18 that she had received Heilner's request on his behalf and explained she recognized the urgency of the matter. She had indeed mentioned the issue to her superiors, but she could not "avoid official restrictions here." She suggested the best way to expedite the request might be for the author to send the museum a very detailed description of the work he planned to do in Cuba (Central Archives, 1216, AMNH). Approximately a week later, Hemingway messaged LaMonte (only in a brief cable, however) to explain his aim with the trip was to "study breeding habits of marlin and broadbill" (March 24, 1943, Central Archives, 1216, AMNH). On the same day, Heilner also cabled LaMonte, insisting the author's work for the museum was going to be "an important contribution to the Department of Ichthyology and [the] Game Fish Association" (March 24, 1943, Central Archives, 1216, AMNH). Albert Eide Parr, the Director of the AMNH, then contacted Hemingway to inform him that "use [of] American Museum flags [is] restricted [to] scientific work under immediate and continuous direction [of the] museum" (March 29, 1943, Central Archives, 1216; AMNH). In short, the answer Hemingway received was a big, fat no because he had not been working closely enough with the museum in the planning stages for officials to be aware of his exact scientific goals.

LaMonte, who was all the while stuck in the middle, then realized her troubles were just beginning, as she was informed that The Office of Censorship, which was set up during World War II to monitor correspondence in and out of the country, flagged her cable to Hemingway on March 18, 1943, as suspicious and requested that she immediately submit an exhaustive description of her comments. On about March 24, 1943, LaMonte provided her superior, Addie Hill Summerson, with a transcript of the cables and her March 22 response to The Office of Censorship's Andrew W. Cruse, who had assumed she was a man considering her profession and had addressed the memo to "Dear Mr. LaMonte." LaMonte's irritation with the matter is on full display. Humorously, LaMonte explained her inclusion of the phrase "understand situation" in order to "mollify Mr. Hemingway and Mr. Heilner, who are both slightly spoiled and slightly temperish and regard any work for the Museum — even although unconfided to any of us — as extremely important and serious." LaMonte revealed the museum could not send its flag and grant credentials without a complete explanation of the activities that will take place during the research. She claimed, "Both Mr. Heilner and Mr. Hemingway ought to have known this." With a final satisfying flourish, she signed her name "(Miss) Francesca LaMonte, Associate Curator, Department of Fishes, Secretary, International Game Fish Association" (LaMonte internal memo, Central Archives, 1216, AMNH).

Apparently, the decision to grant the flag and award credentials was decided by a committee, not by an individual, but Heilner, once he got word of the snub, did not interpret the events that way. In a letter he sent to Hemingway on August 24, 1943, Heilner mentioned that he recently saw Lerner in New York and that they had an argument about the AMNH's decision. Heilner warned he might abandon his IGFA post over the situation, and he inserted Hemingway into the fuss by suggesting he was angry, too (which he may or may not have been). Hemingway's response on September 6, 1943, illustrated his attempt to keep the peace, as he told Heilner to avoid "get[ting] in a jam with" Lerner. He added, "For God's sake don't resign because if you resign I would resign." In a very telling thought, Hemingway pondered what Lerner might be angry about, including that he "never write[s]" and has "not done [his] duty properly" as an officer in the IGFA. Hemingway also implied it was an unrealistic expectation that IGFA business could continue at the same level of rigor even during a time of world war.

Absent of any other knowledge about reasons there may have been tension between Hemingway and Lerner, one could think Hemingway's possible explanations in this letter might be enough to satisfy the situation. However, knowing the lengths Lerner went to in the previous years to get information about the Bimini land from Hemingway, it would make sense he was very frustrated with the author by 1943. Later that fall, Hemingway wrote to Lerner with a request for the "date of purchase and price paid" for the property in 1935 to satisfy paperwork requirements for the Cuban government (Outgoing Correspondence, October 18, 1943, JFK). Lerner did respond with an undated Western Union cable offering the specifics the author needed.

Within the Hemingway archives at the John F. Kennedy Library is a folder for 1941–1958 for Lerner Incoming Correspondence. In it is a terse Western Union cable likely from October 23, 1943, in which Lerner requested to know if Hemingway still possessed the land. If so, he wanted the right to buy it back unless Hemingway had definite plans to build on the lot. (This correspondence was within two months of Heilner notifying Hemingway about the spat with

This photograph illustrates the Bimini docks as they appeared in 1937.

Lerner, which took place sometime between March and August of that year.) A letter from Lerner followed the cable on October 30, 1943, outlining the entire history of their dealings with the property, including Lerner's original purchase price of Hemingway's first plot ($500). This evidence indicates Lerner took a loss on the property in 1935 just to have the author as his neighbor. Lerner also told Hemingway of his abiding desire that he build in Bimini someday. The ending of the letter sounds quite cordial, and apparently Hemingway had invited Lerner to the Finca Vigía for a visit, but Lerner was unable to make the trip because of his busy schedule. A letter from Lerner to Hemingway on January 4, 1944, ribs Hemingway a bit and demonstrates the relationship still had room for playful banter. In extolling the virtues of Bimini life, Lerner said he loved the island so much because he could get away there and not have to fret over things like those who live around him. Just a few letters passed between the two in the following years – including a Merry Christmas telegram Hemingway sent Lerner in December of 1945.

The IGFA Vice Presidential Snafu

It is not until 1949 that a rift may have formed in the Hemingway-Lerner relationship related to Hemingway's reduction in rank of IGFA vice presidents. As the IGFA's success and impact spread across the globe, the need for additional officers arose. By 1945, the IGFA had three vice presidents: Hemingway, Philip Wylie, and Heilner (Rivkin 67). Four years later, in a letter to Lerner on October 23, 1949, Hemingway was livid because his name was dropped in rank in the list of vice presidents in an IGFA publication. Hemingway's main gripe was that one of the men who had been added and named above him ("Papa Montero") was not a skilled fisherman, a fact Hemingway could confirm by having had him on the *Pilar* before. Hemingway feared moves like this would affect the legitimacy and credibility of the IGFA, turning it into what he classified as a "sewing circle." He was also irritated that Wylie, a fisherman and nautical writer who served as an IGFA Field Representative, was listed as the first vice president. Hemingway acknowledged that he was "a little piss-ed off at some of the activities" of the IGFA. Never in any of the letters to Lerner all the way back to 1935 did Hemingway use such a pointed tone.

In a follow-up letter from Lerner to Hemingway marked in handwriting as "after 10/23/49," Lerner tried to contextualize the situation with the naming of the vice presidents by explaining the officers were listed that way due to the layout of the head shots in the publishing process. Lerner also pointed out the whole issue was explained in the minutes of the last meeting, landing a bit of a jab at Hemingway for not reading the IGFA communications, where the reasonable explanation for his concern was found. Lerner then basically told Hemingway that if he wanted to be so involved with the minute details of the IGFA's operation, there was plenty for him to do. He reminded Hemingway there was a backlog of IGFA business waiting to be conducted, and he could certainly be involved in helping clear it. Lerner seems annoyed that Hemingway wanted to play armchair quarterback while avoiding the day-to-day business occupying the time of the other officers. The strain in these exchanges is palpable, though conclusions about any written communications should be drawn very carefully. These letters may not suggest a full falling out of the friendship, but disagreements about the future of the IGFA are clear.

In tricky cases such as this, it is helpful to have the perspective of a Hemingway family member with the ability to shed light on the situation. Hilary Hemingway classifies Hemingway's October 23, 1949, letter as the author "chewing [...] out" Lerner for the listing of the vice presidents. In my opinion, Lerner's irritation with Hemingway's letter was justified. Over the years, a fissure in their relationship could have been growing for a multitude of reasons: Hemingway's less-than-reciprocal letter writing, his refusal to provide answers about the land to Lerner, the author's lack of help as an officer with the IGFA, the fact that he did not return to Bimini with regularity (if at all), and possible suspicion on Hemingway's part that he was being used for promotional purposes. Even so, Hilary Hemingway does not think there was any specific event that caused a falling out between them. She says, "That would have been something my father would have mentioned. [Hemingway] remained good friends with Uncle Mike."

By June 21, 1950, Lerner had clearly tired of the Bimini land situation and Hemingway's apparent refusal to respond to his requests about the deed. Lerner explained how excited he was Hemingway had wanted to build on the lot but suggested the conditions at Bimini (though it is unclear what they were) would prevent the author from ever following through with that intention. He reiterated how his retirement happiness in Bimini and Helen's was at stake and that the idea of having a stranger control the lot would be devastating.

Interestingly, this letter mentions another piece of Bimini property that Lerner sold to Hemingway for $50, apparently before the first lot referenced in the 1935 letters. Supposedly, Lerner made several stock trades for Hemingway and simply subtracted the $50 from the net gain. Lerner then asked for Hemingway to allow him to buy all of the property back for $500 and send him the deed. In an August 22, 1950, letter, Lerner reminded Hemingway of the promise he made to mail the Bimini deed the next time he was in Key West. Hemingway did not follow through with that promise as we will later see.

Much about the land situation comes to light in the February 26, 1951, letter Hemingway wrote to Arthur ("Archie") Gray (Central Archives, 1222.6, AMNH). The reader can infer there had been some miscommunication through a letter and a phone call between Gray and Hemingway about the Bimini land. In this letter, Hemingway informed Gray that if Lerner wanted the property simply to ensure his own view would never be disrupted, the author promised to never sell it. Hemingway claimed his longstanding intention of building a home on the lot and revealed he was "shocked" when Lerner request-ed it back "some time ago." Hemingway told Gray that Lerner had told him the land was going to be used in some way for the Museum, but Lerner had been using the land in the interim as a playground for the native children. Hemingway then promised to confer with his own lawyer to ensure "the property goes to Mike in case I die before he does." Hemingway closed the letter on a very positive note, remarking about how much he appreciated Lerner's friendship.

Lerner wrote on February 6, 1952, that the deed was still not in his possession. The reader can see in this letter that Lerner's patience has run out, and he is desperate to settle the matter. The importance of this land to Lerner is very clear. As a man who had a vast fortune to manage, he devoted so much energy and writing time in his attempt to regain control of a piece of land representing a meager portion of his entire wealth. Thomas Saunders told me that "when Hemingway died, his wife Mary gave [the lot] to the American Museum of Natural History in New York. So, they kept it for a while, and they eventually sold it — after the Lerner Marine Laboratory closed." Because Mary was still in possession of the land after Hemingway's death, the deed never made its way back to Lerner, which had to be terribly disappointing for him.

Another interesting prospect is that Hemingway may have felt he was disappointing Lerner by not getting his "Bimini" narrative published, as it was a tribute to Lerner's wonderful home. Hilary Hemingway explains, "Ernest had wanted *The Old Man [and the Sea]* to have been a part of his larger Sea Book, which maybe he felt at that moment — the Bimini part, set at Lerner's Anchorage home — would never get published. That he had in some way let Lerner down. The worst regrets are not about what we do, as much as what we do not do. It was almost a decade after Ernest's death that *Islands in the Stream* finally saw the light of day." Thomas Hudson's house in *Islands*

This Bimini dock scene is part of the IGFA's Mike Lerner Collection. The IGFA holds the negatives to these photographs, which were likely taken by either Mike or Helen. Because of the number of photographs that exist pertaining to their hunting and fishing expeditions, it can be safely assumed that they traveled with a camera.

is without question Lerner's Anchorage, and Hemingway's inclusion of it in the manuscript may have been his way of thanking Lerner for his friendship, hospitality, and generosity.

The case can be made based on all of this evidence that Hemingway would have felt uncomfortable returning to Bimini in the late 1950s under these circumstances. The last known written correspondence between Hemingway and Lerner was an August 1959 handwritten letter by the author. In it he says he still reminisced about "the old days at Bimini," implying he likely did not go back. When the islanders are asked why they think Hemingway never built on the land, the answers they provide are interesting. Ashley Saunders told me, "Mr. Lerner gave him that property to lure him to Bimini, you know. To kind of like keep him here. But he never really built anything here, because [. . .] I think it is mostly because of his adventuresome life. Hemingway was a person that would not want to be stuck in any one place too long like Bimini. A house meant he'd have to be grounded here." Ansil Saunders's guess is that Hemingway "was just moving too much" at the time. Thomas Saunders agrees Hemingway was "moving around a lot" because he liked to "[follow] the fish around." It is feasible as well that he simply tired of Bimini as he did of Key West and other places in his life. Having houses in both Key West and Cuba, he may have had enough tropical goodness in his life and no longer needed an outlet in Bimini. In my interview with Natty Saunders, when I asked him about why Hemingway never built a house on the King's Highway land, he said, "He was so used to the boat." I finished the idea and asked, "He didn't need another house anywhere?" He responded with an emphatic "No." From my research I have not been able to identify any particular event or blow-up on the island that would have made him reluctant to return.

Hilary Hemingway's earlier point about the timing of the Bimini love affair coinciding with the start of the Gellhorn love affair is germane here as well. He was in those years "focused on changing

wives," she points out, and Martha was focused on charting a new course that would limit any crossover with the travel locations her new love enjoyed with the first two Mrs. Hemingways. As Jimmy Buffett famously said in the seminal "Margaritaville," "Some people claim there's a woman to blame." This explanation seems to suit here as well as any other. Even so, when you have seen the King's Highway land in person, it is hard to imagine how anyone could rationalize letting it go to waste. In my opinion, if new buyers come to town for the property, every penny they spend will be worth it. Maybe one day I will save enough pennies to own it myself.

The house was built on the highest part of the narrow tongue of land between the harbor and the open sea. It had lasted through three hurricanes and it was built solid as a ship. It was shaded by tall coconut palms that were bent by the trade wind and on the ocean side you could walk out of the door and down the bluff across the white sand and into the Gulf Stream.

— Hemingway, *Islands in the Stream*

VII

The Hemingway Legacy in Bimini

JUST NINE YEARS after Hemingway's death in 1961, his widow Mary and publisher Charles Scribner decided to release *Islands in the Stream*, the novel that would immortalize Bimini in the Hemingway canon and a book that to this day makes the native islanders extraordinarily proud. The novel was released on October 6, 1970, and *Esquire* helped promote the work by printing a 34,000-word excerpt of the "Bimini" section for its October 1970 issue. Michael Hemmingson discloses in "*Esquire's* Failure with Hemingway's 'Bimini'" that the story was "published with a hope that the appearance of a posthumous Hemingway work would boost the magazine's diminishing sales and stature in the literary community" (140). The Editor's Note accompanying the excerpt opens with a series of questions related to the posthumous release of a major author's unfinished book: "As the manuscript stands, does it represent the author's intentions at the peak of his skills? If by conventional standards it does not, should the work nevertheless be put forward? Given the choice, would the author knowingly have consented to its later publication? Or, given the demands of history to know the full scope of his work, should the author's assumed preference be a factor in any case?" (Hemingway, "Bimini" 121). The Editor's Note is an attempt to preemptively squelch the criticism for posthumous publication the publisher and Mary knew had to be coming, and the fact that these specific questions were even posed suggests to me

The October 1970 edition of *Esquire* magazine, which included the "Bimini" section of the forthcoming novel *Islands in the Stream*.

the folks working on the project were aware the answers were not going to be favorable. No, *Islands in the Stream* does not represent Hemingway's intentions at the peak of his skills. Since the book does not meet his standards, it should not have been released anyway. Hemingway likely would not have consented to its later publication because he did not consent to its publication while he was alive, and he had the manuscript in his possession for a decade before he died. Because the answers to the first three questions were a resounding no, the response to the last query must be yes: Hemingway's preference should matter. If the author thought the work was a masterpiece, he would have pulled the trigger and sent it to a publisher while he was alive, as he did with so many books that felt finished to him. Likewise, if *Esquire*'s editor thought the work was a masterpiece, he would not have hedged his bet in the preface to the magazine's excerpt.

Even though the book as a whole is not Hemingway's best effort, of all that he left to the Bimini community, *Islands* stands as his greatest and most tangible gift. The first of the three sections, called "Bimini," is captivating — by far the best part of the novel. The second section is set in Cuba and the third on the open ocean off the coast of Cuba. Reading the opening section, I am struck by the mastery with which Hemingway put into words the stunning beauty of the King's Highway perch of the Anchorage looking out over Radio Beach and the majestic Gulf Stream in the distance. Hemingway captures the essence of the place so perfectly it is hard to imagine any writer doing a better job. You might not like the book's structure, perhaps you have trouble connecting to the storyline, but you cannot deny the delicacy and accuracy of the Bimini descriptions. The novel chronicles a snapshot of the life of Thomas Hudson, a painter who comes to the island for solitude but then faces the death of his two young sons. The first segment of the book is set in the 1930s on the island. The contrast of the allure of Bimini with the crushing emotional blow Hudson endures is devastating for the reader who gets involved in the story, and despite the fact that most critics suggest it is difficult for the reader to become invested in the events of Hudson's life, I find him to be a very interesting (if not fully complete) character.

Unfortunately, the way *Islands* came together can only be classified as problematic. The author's participation in the publication of any piece of fiction is essential if the true vision of the work is to be maintained in the final product. Readers can obviously analyze the text however they wish after publication, but those interpretations follow from knowing the author's intent for the work was honored. Because of the questionable nature of the novel's production, it is essentially impossible for readers or critics to get their bearings. Joseph M. DeFalco argues in "'Bimini' and the Subject of Hemingway's *Islands in the Stream*" that "even if the novel were a finished product, the likelihood of its having received critical acclaim is remote," mainly due to the unclear nature of the novel's subject (42). It appears Hem-

This happy welcome sign greets visitors to Bimini and proudly claims the name of "The Island in the Stream."

ingway intended to produce a trilogy: one book each about the sea, the land, and the air. The full air and land books never happened (though parts of the land book turned into *Across the River and Into the Trees*). The "Sea Novel" or "Sea Book" evolved into *The Old Man and the Sea* and *Islands in the Stream*. Hendrickson reports, "In the summer of 1951, Hemingway put a microfilm copy of sixteen hundred pages of the unfinished Sea Book into a lockbox at the Banco Nacional of Havana, keeping the original for revisions, but apparently he didn't work on it again after December 1951" (286). Hemingway still intended to revise the book, and he was the only qualified person for the task. The image the Editor's Note conjures of "Mrs. Hemingway and her associates [. . .] preparing the manuscript for its final form" is wrong in every way (121).

The Old Man and the Sea, which netted Hemingway a deserved Pulitzer Prize in 1953 and a Nobel Prize in Literature the following year, was released in 1952 with the author's approval, and it stands in my estimation as his crowning literary achievement. The fact that *Islands* was published in spite of its unfinished state makes it a very difficult book to appraise. As expected, critical analysis of the work began in earnest shortly after its release in 1970. In my view, it is best to enjoy the book for what it is (a glimpse into Hemingway's vision for a book that was unfortunately altered by other people) instead of getting all twisted up about what it lacks. Criticism of a dead author's incomplete work seems like the worst sort of sucker punch. I find the most value from *Islands* critics who make a concerted effort to note the positives about the novel and to analyze the many negatives mercifully. DeFalco writes, "The critical judgment of *Islands in the Stream* as a work riddled with defects is largely correct" while still noting his "attempt to shift [. . .] emphasis to the subject of the 'sea' and away from character in order to engage themes larger than the human personality was an impressive experiment" (51). If

Mary insisted upon publishing it, the manuscript should have been released as Hemingway left it. Since it was determined the text was not suitable for release as it was, it should have been cataloged in the Hemingway Collection at the John F. Kennedy Library as an unfinished manuscript. Walter Houk's supremely interesting "A Sailor Looks at Hemingway's *Islands*" points out that the title is not even right: "Hemingway's own title, 'The Island and the Stream,' referred to Bimini, beside (not *in*) the Gulf Stream. [. . .] But the published title, though intended to account for the novel's other islands, failed to notice that they were not in the Stream either. [. . .] [T]here are in fact no islands in the Gulf Stream" (16). Embarrassing errors like this one are to be expected when people who are not artists and who cannot possibly know the full creative plan of the writer who initiated the project attempt to tie up what they see as loose ends.

Hemingway's writing honored the places he truly loved by preserving them as they were in the moment he experienced them, and it is fitting that Bimini now stands alongside Key West, Cuba, Paris, many locales in Italy and Spain, and others too numerous to mention. Bimini is what it is because Hemingway was there, and the wonderful people of the island really would not have it any other way. The argument can easily be supported that the most interesting era in Bimini history was ushered in the very day the *Pilar* pulled into port in 1935. Hemingway's presence there, his subsequent work with the IGFA, and his writing about the island were the instruments largely responsible for shaping the delightful culture that exists today. No matter what you think of the book itself, *Islands in the Stream* keeps Hemingway's legacy alive in Bimini. You can hear the excitement about the novel in the voices of the natives who are so eager to talk about it, and some will not hesitate to quote passages from the text if asked. Ansil Saunders classifies Hemingway as "the greatest writer of fish and marine things. He had that gift of writing in a way that made it hard to put the book down. He would make the story so enchanting that you couldn't wait to see what happened." What an honor to have your beloved home forever preserved in a book by a superior literary craftsman who adored the island himself.

The Queen's Highway is populated almost exclusively by bicycles, scooters, and golf carts. Renting a golf cart to explore the island is a wise choice. Having transportation on the island will facilitate your morning trips to A Taste of Heaven Bakery, a perfect little pastry shop that lives up to its moniker in every way.

Important Historical Sites

Bimini today truly is a place where the tired cliché "time has stood still" applies in many ways. To a researcher visiting the island for the sole purpose of following the Hemingway trail, it was quite surprising to find a place not that far removed from the iconic black-and-white photographs of the 1930s. The Lerners' Anchorage property is nestled on top of the hill, the home itself in remarkably good shape considering the harsh island elements. The white paint with cheerful Bimini blue trim makes it both contrast and connect with the sea spread out at its doorstep. The Anchorage now serves as a hotel and restaurant, and walking into the dining room in the main house, the visitor who understands what incredible houseguests the home welcomed is overcome by the sense of the structure's history.

A quick stroll around the main house and to the rest of the grounds leads to the "Blue Marlin Cottage," where Pauline and the

The "Blue Marlin Cottage" on the Anchorage property is now rented out by Blue Water Resort.

The Lerners' magnificent Anchorage was built by Ashley, Ansil, and Thomas Saunders's father in the 1930s.

The Anchorage bar is an inviting place to come in from the tropical heat and enjoy a cocktail.

Hemingway sons sometimes resided when they were on the island. The cottage is now rented out by the Blue Water Resort, though the structure is "much changed" since the Hemingways stayed there in the 1930s (Sandra Davis, "Marlin Cottage"). Being able to lodge in any part of the historic Lerner property would be a special treat. The Anchorage compound includes a striking set of shrubbery-lined steps that unfold down the hill, the same steps Mike Lerner surely took to work at the Lerner Marine Laboratory on the Queen's Highway. The whole complex still exudes the feeling that very special things happened there.

The main building for the lab still stands today. The facility (now painted bright pink) is currently being used as government offices for everything from the postal service to immigration, though a commemorative plaque explaining the site's significance has been erected. Right across the street, you can look out over the harbor and see where the Lerner Lab's docks and live wells used to be. The scientists who were lucky enough to be stationed there had the opportunity to participate in such extraordinary research, much of which was published. Today interested readers can search online auction websites and find Lerner Marine Lab anthologies containing findings and conference proceedings.

Bimini Shark Lab

While there is no organizational connection between the two efforts, the Bimini Shark Lab is continuing cutting-edge shark research in the absence of the Lerner Marine Laboratory. Located on South Bimini, the Bimini Biological Field Station was opened in 1990 by Dr. Samuel Gruber from the University of Miami. The scientists in residence are happy to tell visitors about their most current research, and going there may make you want to abandon your career, devote your life to marine study, and move to Bimini. During my trip, we

The former Lerner Marine Laboratory site now houses Bahamian
government offices. Notice the blue historical marker to the
right of the central walkway.

The Lerner Marine Laboratory docks and live wells were right across the street
from the facility's offices. No evidence of the structures remains in the water.

were invited out to the Field Station's live wells to hear about ongoing projects related to fascinating topics like the differences in shark personalities. You should call ahead to schedule a tour time and be sure to make a donation to compensate the scientists for their time and to support their important work.

All visitors to Bimini should take the time to stop by the Bimini Shark Lab. If you are lodging on North Bimini, a ferry runs between the two islands at regular intervals.

The Compleat Angler, where Hemingway stayed in the 1930s in Room One on the second floor and where a fabulous Hemingway Museum was housed, burned down on January 13, 2006, killing owner Julian Brown and ravaging a large collection of Hemingway photographs and relics. Bimini Museum Director Sir Michael Checkley said of the tragedy, "This was the major landmark on the island and it's just completely destroyed — it's like Rome without the Vatican now" ("Bimini Compleat Angler Burned Down"). Regrettably, I was unable to visit the island before the disaster; therefore, I am forced to rely on the remembrances of others and the old photographs to imagine the atmosphere of the space. By far the best published reminiscence of the historic hotel is "The View from the Verandah: The Hemingway Room at the Compleat Angler" by H. R. "Stoney" Stoneback, a scholar who most would agree is the preeminent living Hemingway resource. His remembrances about the hotel and the Hemingway Room he helped to create, when juxtaposed with the horror of the fire, will rip your heart out. Visiting the ruins of the great hotel today is very somber indeed. If you are on the Queen's Highway heading south in Alice Town, you will see the remnants of the great fireplace towering above the site.

What is left of The Compleat Angler Hotel after the fire that destroyed it on January 13, 2006. Owner Julian Brown died after heroically attempting to warn hotel guests about the danger.

The remains of the grand fireplace are a sad sight.
A great Hemingway museum was lost to the fire.

Without question, the biggest physical change to happen on the island since Hemingway's time is the construction of a cruise ship pier in September 2014. Shortly thereafter, Hilton opened phase one of Resorts World Bimini, a luxury hotel and rental home complex complete with a casino, restaurants, shops, and boat docks. The construction was opposed by the islanders, but the battle with developers was eventually lost. The resort provides the most posh hotel accommodations on the island. The dock was home to the Bimini SuperFast cruise ship, which brought tourists to the island several times each week from Miami. Prior to 2014 (before a large cruise ship was capable of docking), a tender boat system was used to ferry passengers from larger ships that anchored offshore (DiPano). Outside of the Hilton's development of the northern end of North Bimini, new construction is not a fact of everyday life on the island, and that seems to suit the islanders just fine.

However, in January 2016, the *Miami Herald* reported the Resorts World Bimini SuperFast cruises from Miami to Bimini were permanently suspended. I was actually on the very last cruise out of Bimini on January 10, 2016. *Miami Herald* writer Marjie Lambert revealed that since the cruise service started in 2013, "the number of visitors to Bimini doubled to 117,315 in 2014, the first full year that Genting's casino and ferry were in operation." The article explains that in 2013, air travel options to the island were not consistent. Since

The *Bimini SuperFast* sits at the dock just before her last commute back to America in January 2016.

then, two airlines — Cape Air and Silver Airways — have added many more daily flight options. When asked, the islanders have heard different stories about the future of cruises to Bimini. Some think jumbo cruise liners are on the way. Large ships coming to the Bahamas from America could make Bimini the first or last port of call. The passage and docking of larger cruise ships would likely require the dredging of the channel, which would be harmful to wildlife and habitats. Quite frankly, the docking of larger cruise ships would kill more than wildlife; it would destroy the ambiance of the island. An additional concern is Bimini's total lack of infrastructure to support thousands of day-tripping tourists at a time. One only has to be in Old Town Key West when the cruise ships let off passengers to see what this kind of activity does to a quaint place, and Key West was far better situated than Bimini will ever be to handle the cruise ship masses. Others have heard a ship closer in size to the Bimini SuperFast might take up the route. Lambert's article cites sources at Resorts World Bimini who say "a more efficient ferry operation" will be established in 2016. Until the new options are up and running, there is no question the economy of Bimini will suffer. Several Biminites I interviewed suggested the stoppage could possibly be attributed to election politics, and contracts are likely being renegotiated among officials.

Beyond this current economic reality, though, is the extraordinarily important fact that history is *alive* for Biminites, and Hemingway is central to that consciousness. As I stood in Ansil Saunders's Boat House one sunny afternoon, he told me, "In the minds of the people here, Hemingway never died. [...] Hemingway's life in Bimini is something that will never die." When I asked native Cleveland Francis about whether the people of Bimini still talk about Hemingway, his response was incredibly sincere and touching: "Of course. They miss him." Thomas Saunders agrees, saying Hemingway "meant something to the people." Even years later, Hemingway's footprints are still everywhere and his impact is unmistakable.

My experiences on the island confirmed the way the "extended present," like the one regarded by the Native American oral tradition, is very much a part of the Bimini sensibility. Even the distant past, known within the Native American worldview as "time immemorial," is perceived as vitally connected to present existence. As a person who has spent considerable time in Key West (both for research and for pleasure), I can say that island's particular marketing machine has become very proficient at keeping Hemingway's *memory* alive. With its corny drinks, hokey T-shirts, and look-alike contests, Key West's portrayal of Hemingway is one that is situated firmly in the *past*. One does not walk around the streets of Key West and meet people who knew Hemingway. His house is there, but he is not. When walking the streets of Bimini, one can ask any passerby, no matter his or her age, "Do you know about Ernest Hemingway?" and they will *all* say, "Oh yeah, Mr. Hemingway." The young ones will say, "You need to

Bimini scholar Ashley Saunders stands in front of the splendid Dolphin House Museum and shop on Saunders Street.

talk to my grandfather." Those of advanced years will say, "Yes, I met him" or "I was just too young to remember him when he was here, but I know all about him." Ashley Saunders, the curator of the Dolphin House Museum, says Hemingway is "just below Jesus, when it comes right down to it, [as far as] his legacy, and he will live on for generations to come on this island. His name is synonymous with Bimini." To have an actual point of reference to contrast the way Hemingway is *remembered* in Key West and the way his persona *exists* in Bimini is indispensable to the Hemingway scholar and the historian.

When interviewing subjects such as Ashley, Ansil, Thomas, and Natty Saunders, one gets the sense that they have delivered these Hemingway stories many, many times. More often than not, interviewers are asked to pay for access to the folks who know the stories or to buy the goods they are selling. Scholars and journalists on Bimini have documented this phenomenon before. While many would scoff at this practice, I think it is at least partly a testament to how much Biminites value the experiences they had. There is no question they are proud of their heritage, and they are honored to have Hemingway connections. Once involved in these storytelling sessions, the orators do not want visitors to get away from the conversations until they have told them everything. They want other people to know Bimini's history, too. There is a rhythm and a pattern to the stories and the speakers are particular that the narratives unfold in a precise, controlled way. Interjecting with questions will not divert their focus, so the listener quickly learns to sit back and follow along. The stories will not end until the speaker is finished with the cycle. The listener is just along for the delightful ride. Likewise, the delivery of the stories is very rehearsed and performative, again the result of the great pride the speakers have for their experiences. Many of the natives are quick to pull out all of the Hemingway-related books they own. Thomas has a notebook log with one-line subjects. For each subject, there is a story, and the interested visitor can simply ask him to expound on one and enjoy the narrative. He showed me newspaper clippings, copies of the Bimini newsletter written by Leicester Hemingway and a book signed by a Hemingway family member. Ansil retrieved a book autographed by Coretta Scott King, and he had his copy of Paul Hendrickson's *Hemingway's Boat* handy in the Boat Shop. Similarly, the Dolphin House Museum is full of Hemingway reference books.

Considering the very limited resources and the minute population of Bimini, the fact that two museums (The Bimini Heritage Museum and The Dolphin House Museum) exist is remarkable. For such a small island, where the funding for museums and historical preservation is nothing like what is available in America, Bimini has done an immense job of capturing its history. Historical markers are absolutely everywhere on North Bimini, along with many memorials and plaques. These markers are even more vital after the loss of The Compleat Angler Hemingway Museum. There is a healthy move-

The Bimini Museum opened in 2000. The structure where the museum is housed was built in the 1920s during American Prohibition (Davis, "Bimini Museum & Heritage Center").

ment on the island to make sure its heritage is never forgotten, and for that historians should rejoice.

Hemingway's history on the island is remembered in this Bimini Heritage informational placard.

All aging generations worry the youngsters coming behind them will not treasure the past in the way the people who lived the history would prefer. The general consensus among the old guard of Biminites is that younger folks on the island are not as connected to the past as they could or should be. Ansil Saunders says after Hemingway left the island, "the era changed. What was important 40 years before the young folks got here isn't important to them." The generation with direct access to Hemingway is quickly fading out. Ashley Saunders acknowledges, "All of those guys have passed on in. Carlos Gutiérrez died. Then Joe Bain. Manny Rolle ("Mr. Chair Boy") and also Cephas Davis — they all died. Only my Uncle Nat Saunders [is] left — Piccolo Pete." He continues, "The only person living now that really remembers Hemingway in any detail [. . .] is my uncle, Nat Saunders."

The generation in between Natty Saunders and the youngsters coming into their own now, though, has done a terrific job of preserving the details of Hemingway's life on the island so that when the younger folks are ready to plug in, it will all be there waiting. Ashley Saunders has worked tirelessly to ensure this transition takes place: "My son, I've already got him trained to keep the Dolphin House Museum going on. The Museum will be open and running just the way it is running right now. We want to keep this going for generations to come. The Dolphin House is a house that is never to be sold. It is all to keep the Hemingway legacy, the island history, and culture intact. This is actually a Bahamian national treasure, so we would want to continue with the Dolphin House and museum and everything like it is." A visit to the Dolphin House should be at the top of your to-do list, and if you are lucky, Ashley Saunders might allow you inside the home to see his spectacular architectural designs and interior decorations. Through his use of found objects, he has adorned nearly every square inch of the interior with shells, glass, tiles, and too many other materials to mention. The house, which is available for rent, has to be the most interesting place to stay on the island and would be well worth the rental fee.

As the first scholar ready to pull the trigger and write the Hemingway book about Bimini, I was taken aback that no one had ever undertaken the project before me. (I have a tendency to become frustrated upon discovering a book I want to read has not been written, and I sign up for the task.) The academics participating in the field of Hemingway studies have a vested interest in the author's history on the island. Those who have written on the topic before me shared my enthusiasm for the people and the place. The relative lack of island infrastructure (especially before the construction of the Hilton) is perhaps the reason an academic conference dedicated to Hemingway

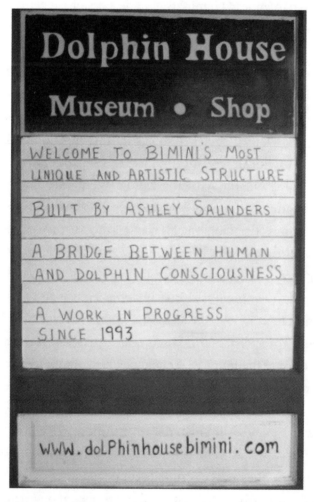

The door of the Dolphin House Museum announces that the artistic vision for the structure has been evolving since 1993.

did not take place on the island until January 1995. That is the year six members of the Hemingway Society held the first Nick Adams Convocation. Robert Gadjusek, Will Watson, Allen Josephs, Stoney and Sparrow Stoneback, and Don Junkins were the scholars in attendance. The event was designed to honor the 60th anniversary of Hemingway's first visit to the island (Saunders, *Volume 1*, 34). Gadjusek said of the experience, "The love of the native islanders for Hemingway is deep, memories are still fresh, and we were generously invited into homes" ("'New' Bimini Museum" 2). In 2000, the Hemingway Society held the International Hemingway Conference on the island from January 3–9, 2000. Scholars met at both The Compleat Angler and the Bimini Big Game Club. Junkins was the organizer and Natty Saunders was in attendance.

Famous Faces

Providentially, after Hemingway's glory days on the island, Bimini's parade of intriguing characters did not end. Hemingway's younger brother, Leicester, spent the last few years of his life on the island before he committed suicide in 1982. As was mentioned in the opening chapter, Leicester was also on the island to search for the elusive Fountain of Youth. Hilary Hemingway told me her father worked in Bimini "from 1968 until a month before his death. He ran two newspapers, the *Bimini-Bugle* followed by the *Bimini-News*. I spent most of my teen years helping him with the leg work, distributing his newspaper towards the end of his life. Honestly, I had no idea what a great life it was going to Bimini for the weekends." She revealed, "My dad gave a lot of love to Bimini folks, and those who knew him loved him, too." Despite the sad ending to his fascinating life, his daughter says Leicester "raised four good kids, had wonderful adventures, and treated my mom as a queen. [...] We lived in a great house and drove old cars, and we were happy."

Dr. Martin Luther King, Jr., the civil rights pioneer and the most skilled American orator of the last century, came to Bimini on more than one occasion to rest, think, and compose. In 1964, he wrote his acceptance speech for the Nobel Peace Prize on the island, and in 1968 (just days before his assassination in Memphis, Tennessee), he crafted the Sanitation Workers speech in Bimini. Ansil Saunders is renowned on the island for taking Dr. King out in his skiff. The story goes that Dr. King wanted a serene place to work on what regrettably turned out to be the last speech he delivered, and Ansil agreed to pilot his boat to a quiet place. If you are ever in Bailey Town and have an opportunity to stop by Ansil's Boat House, you will not be disappointed in his storytelling. Visiting the King Center and burial site in Atlanta, Georgia, is a wonderful experience, but hearing a man who was with Dr. King at such a pivotal moment in history tell his story (all while standing next to the very boat the two used to go out on

Ansil Saunders sits on the skiff he used to take Dr. Martin Luther King, Jr. out on the water for a time of reflection right before the civil rights leader's death.

the water on that famous day) will make history come authentically alive. For this reason, Dr. King's legacy on the island is still very much a part of the present instead of the past, and the people celebrate and revere their connection to him.

For this writer, all things circle back to Jimmy Buffett in one way or another, and the Bimini story is no different. Buffett came to the island frequently in the 1980s and 1990s, which makes sense because Bimini felt an awful lot like Margaritaville to me. He would arrive on his seaplane and park at the Chalk's Seaplane Ramp, which was on the very south side of North Bimini, very close to where the King's Highway ends (south of Weech's dock). During those years, he was heavily involved in composing a quick succession of wonderful books, though it is unclear exactly how much writing he did in Bimini. We

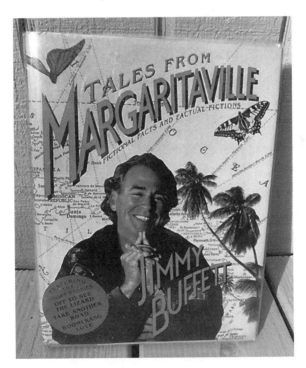

The foreword of Jimmy Buffett's outstanding *Tales from Margaritaville* was written in Bimini. In addition to being one of the great songwriters of our time, Buffett is also a fine novelist and short story author.

know for sure he was in Bimini when he wrote the foreword to *Tales from Margaritaville* (my favorite book of the 1980s), as it famously mentions his exploits on the island. Buffett currently owns a house on a neighboring isle, and he continues to go fishing in Bimini. In fact, he hired my charter guide just four months before I did on my trip in early 2016. Aside from the annual concerts, this was sadly as close to Mr. Buffett as I will likely ever be.

Bimini's present state is much like its past in that the doses of good are often tempered by the bad. Unfortunately, drug activity over the last decades has to an extent disrupted the tranquility of Bimini. Especially in the 1980s, "drug drops" were a massive problem in the islands. Traffickers used airplanes to drop large bundles of illegal drugs into waiting boats. While officials had good luck stopping the boats engaged in this activity, catching the airplanes making the drops was nearly impossible. Newspaper archives from the 1980s suggest South Bimini was once completely overtaken by drug smugglers. Evidence of Bimini's unfortunate part in the drug trade is still visible in the landscape. While fishing offshore, our party drove past a partially submerged drug plane that crashed and was abandoned many years ago. Just as in America, drug activity is part of Bimini life, and drug seizures (some of them on a very large scale) still occur. One of the fabulous yachts I saw docked in the harbor had just been part of a huge cocaine bust. The synopsis about Bimini on Frommer's Online reveals that "because of its proximity to the mainland, Bimini, as is no secret to anyone, is now a major drop-off point for drugs, many originating from Colombia" ("Fast Facts: Bimini"). Chapter I outlined the characteristics of the island that made Bimini so appealing to pirates and rumrunners, so it is no surprise that nefarious activity has continued in the area and evolved over time.

The remains of an abandoned drug plane are an unexpected discovery for the first-time Bimini visitor.

The Big-Game Fishing Economy

Big-game fishing became a permanent part of the island after the 1930s, and its economic impact is still felt. Fishing remains "the backbone of our island's economy," according to Ashley Saunders. He reminds the listener that Hemingway "brought big-game fishing to Bimini and the big-game fishing industry to Bimini [...], so I would think that [this is] his greatest contribution." In an interview with Tim McDonald for an article in the *Los Angeles Times*, Saunders explained, "You take Hemingway away from Bimini and there's nothing left." The number of available quality fishing captains compared to the number of actual Bimini residents is astounding. Any number of world-class bonefishing guides are available for flats fishing, and reef and offshore excursions are also very popular. Anglers who want an

One of the barracuda I hooked while trolling in the Gulf Stream with Captain Ebbie David. If you only had one day in Paris, you would visit the Eiffel Tower. It follows that if you only have a day in Bimini, you should go fishing.

offshore fishing charter might be surprised in Bimini when they realize they do not have to travel very far in a boat to reach the extraordinarily deep waters of the Gulf Stream, an added bonus for fishermen and fisherwomen who are prone to seasickness like this writer. My own offshore fishing outing with Captain "Bonefish Ebbie" David was brilliant, even though I did not hook into a world-record bluefin tuna or marlin. John Bell reports in "Bimini Beckons" the island is "home today to some 50 world-record catches and counting" (37), all the more reason to book your charter and hope that today is your lucky world-record day.

The Bimini Big Game Club includes a very satisfying gift shop and a relaxing outdoor grill with spectacular views of the water.

The Bimini Big Game Club, which was central to the island's hospitality to visiting anglers from around the world from the day Neville Stuart opened it in 1936, unfortunately closed in 2009 due to financial distress. Luckily, conservationist and artist Guy Harvey purchased the property and reopened it as a Guy Harvey Outpost on July 21, 2010, a day that would have been Hemingway's 75th birthday

Fish replicas decorate the walkway at the beautiful Bimini Big Game Club.

(Bell 37). The club offers a gorgeous marina and a most satisfying place to have dinner on the island. Aside from the nice accommodations, it is comforting that a conservationist view has really taken hold in Bimini. Bell wrote, "Though the Bimini of Hemingway, Grey and Lerner lives on as both legend and recorded history, today's Bimini exists in a more delicately balanced world where eco-systems and bio-diversity are considerations when promoting traditional pursuits such as fishing, diving and boating" (37). In a bold and wonderful move in 2011, the Bahamas actually banned all commercial shark fishing, and now only catch and release of sharks is allowed. I suspect the early fishermen who put Bimini on the fishing map would be very pleased with these developments that will safeguard the island's splendid natural resources.

The new and improved Bimini Big Game Club also includes Hemingway's Rum Bar and Social Lounge. The bar, which was built around the club's original watering hole, is part of the Gulfstream

Conference Center project ("Guy Harvey's"). Hilary Hemingway donated dozens of photographs in the name of her father for the project.
She also contributed "a hundred copies of the *Bimini-News* because
the issues document events in Bimini during the '70s and '80s. After
the Court House burned down in the early 1980s, the island lost its
records of births, marriages, and deaths." The bar's walls are covered
with fishing memorabilia and photographs, and any angler on the
island should stop in for a quick visit.

The monster fish Hemingway and his colleagues caught in
abundance at Bimini are not as common now, and the Bimini fishing
grounds stand as yet another example of humans messing up a really
good thing. Commercial fishing has had an impact on Bimini's environment. Once again, Farrington prophetically wrote in 1971 that
commercial longline fishing is "so simple and efficient that it could
conceivably strip the world's best fishing grounds of all game fish"

Watching the boats returning with their catches during peak fishing season is a
fabulous way to spend a Bimini evening.

(*Fishing with Hemingway and Glassell* 35). Speaking in a 1985 article for *Motor Boating and Sailing* magazine, Bonnie Waitzkin argued the bygone days of Hemingway and Company will never happen again "because such abundance of big marine life is a thing of the past" unless one travels to a location like Australia (70). She went on to remind the reader of the changed ethical mindset that has filtered into the sport, noting that anglers today would not dream of bringing to the dock the huge fish who have somehow managed to "survive the long liners and the oil slicks" (70). As with all great fishing fields on the planet, only a global conservation effort is going to protect the finite resources of the ocean. If the great fish ever left Bimini, it would be a disaster of epic proportions. Because of the conservation work of groups like the IGFA, catch and release has finally become part of the consciousness of fishermen (both amateur and professional). This is a monumental shift from the days when thousands of pounds of abandoned game fish sat spoiling on the shore after the celebratory photographs were snapped.

Hemingway's fishing legacy still survives in a number of ways in Bimini. In 1993, the Bimini Fishing Hall of Fame was born. Six people, including Hemingway, Lerner, and Farrington, were inducted in the inaugural class (Saunders *Volume 1*, 34). Fishing tournaments are also big business on the island, with the Bimini Hemingway Festival and Fishing Tournament taking place annually. Hemingway family members also make it back to Bimini from time to time to fish in the tournaments. In 2013, Hemingway's grandson John fished in the Wahoo Smackdown II as he was on assignment for *Sport Fishing Magazine* (Frey). Interestingly, Hilary Hemingway reports her uncle "didn't like fishing tournaments. It doesn't take as much skill to win a fishing tournament; it takes luck." Her quote reminds me of Santiago's poignant reflection about luck versus skill as he battled his great marlin. He thinks to himself, "But who knows? Maybe today. Every day is a new day. It is better to be lucky. But I would rather be exact. Then when luck comes you are ready" (*The Old Man and the Sea* 32).

Even though he may not have been a fan of fishing tournaments, Hemingway participated in them, and he helped organize the first Ernest Hemingway Billfishing Tournament in Havana. The inaugural event was held in May of 1950, and Hemingway won, representing the International Yacht Club of Havana. He went on to collect the championship in the next two years as well. In a fascinating coincidence, Fidel Castro participated in and won the 1960 tournament, the legitimacy of his award "being confirmed by guests onboard the *Pilar* who kept *El Presidente* under close binocular scrutiny" (German). The subsequent meeting of Hemingway and Castro during the

One of my favorite Goodwill finds: a framed photograph of the famous 1960 meeting between Hemingway and Fidel Castro after the dictator won the annual Ernest Hemingway Billfishing Tournament. Despite holding three trophies, Castro still managed to hang on to his Cuban cigar.

awards ceremony was the only known time they ever met. The 66th edition of the fishing classic will take place in June 2016.

IGFA world records are constantly changing as anglers continue their quest to make history. Over the years dozens of fishing records have been broken in and around Bimini. The IGFA's outstanding on-line search engine allows members to scan the records by line class, species, angler name, and country. These days Bimini is still very famous for its bonefishing tradition, and the island holds the all-tackle world record for a 16-pound bonefish caught by Jerry Lavenstein in 1971 with Ansil Saunders as his guide. Notably, golfer Sam Snead caught a 15-pound bonefish in Bimini in 1953 while fishing with the legendary guide "Bonefish Willie" Duncombe (Craig Davis). While not a world record, the only 1,000-pound blue marlin ever caught in the Bahamas was taken in Bimini. It happened during the 2011 Bahamas Billfish Championship. David Albury fought the fish for three hours before bringing the 1,119-pound blue marlin to the scales (Hudson). The all-tackle record for cero/king mackerel (18 pounds) was caught by Jimmy Wickett in Bimini in 2013. A Guy Harvey Outpost blog entry in November 2010 announced four world records were broken by the same husband-wife team, Martin and Roberta Arostegui, on a two-day fishing trip in Bimini ("Four New IGFA Records Set in Bimini"). This small selection of notable contemporary Bimini catches demonstrates the impact the island still has on the larger world of sport fishing today.

Hemingway believed all fishing records were meant to be broken. His fishing résumé (especially considering the tackle he used and the virgin waters he explored) has to be included among the best of all time: the 786-pound mako shark just 12 pounds short of the world record, the day in 1938 when he set a world record by boating seven marlin, the 119-pound Atlantic sailfish record, and blue marlin over 500 pounds. Even today, the world record for the Atlantic sailfish is

142 pounds, just 23 pounds more than Hemingway's fish. In *Hemingway in Love*, A. E. Hotchner remembers Hemingway telling him about "the time he and Hadley had the incredible luck of catching sixteen marlins in one string of days, and how that feat meant more to him than netting the Pulitzer Prize" (142). Like so many anglers before and after him, he was endlessly entertained by the prospect of what the next day might bring, and by all accounts he rose early to be out on the water and ready for the challenge.

The Hemingway mystique will likely continue to grow on the island even as the generations become further removed from the author's actual years there. From a scholarly perspective, there has been renewed interest in Hemingway because of the United States normalizing diplomatic relationships with Cuba in July 2015. By February 2016, the establishment of commercial flights between the two countries was already in the news. As a result, we have seen a flurry of articles about Hemingway and new enthusiasm for his biography.

Mark Rogers writes, "The current thaw in relations between Cuba and the United States and an influx of tourists from the U.S. has re-ignited interest in Hemingway's connection to Cuba, and in turn, his connections to [. . .] Key West and Bimini." Hopefully, these political changes and the publication of this book will keep the spotlight on Bimini, a deserving little island inhabited by some of the most enter-taining people I have ever met. May Bimini's tomorrows be as lively and unpredictable as its yesterdays.

"Dr. O, that book was awesome. I've never
actually liked reading a story before."

A Pfeiffer University sophomore after reading
The Old Man and the Sea for the first time

Afterword

In closing my last book, I reflected on the great privilege it is to
visit the beach. As I conclude this work, I am grateful for the
opportunity to write about the most resplendent place on the
earth I have ever beheld and for the chance to travel to that island
paradise to document it. I am thankful as well to Pineapple Press for
giving me this platform to present some of the most extraordinary
aspects of Hemingway's life. For years I have been frustrated by the
mean-spirited and often baseless criticism that only appears interested in attacking and not understanding him. It is fruitless to judge
a writer who lived so long ago using today's standards as the bench-
mark. In reality, it is fruitless to judge others at all, a truth that applies
especially when critics are writing about authors they never met and
whose life experiences they can only access in letters, books, articles,
and photographs. Kip Farrington saw the tidal wave of negativity
coming only 10 years after Hemingway's death as he wrote in the
foreword to *Fishing with Hemingway and Glassell*: "His reputation,
for me, remains vivid and whole in spite of the best efforts of the

literary sharks to tear him to shreds and drag him down" (vii–viii). Maybe more Hemingway scholars will publish books like this one — realistic about the man but without a venomous critical axe to grind.

As a student who went straight from high school through an undergraduate degree, a Masters, and a Ph.D. (completing the doctorate in 2007), I was only required to read *one* Hemingway text: *The Sun Also Rises* at the doctoral level. Sadly, his works do not find their way into the classroom with regularity anymore. Of all the writers included on my current university syllabi, my students are most drawn to Hemingway's work. His writing and his incredible biography have the power to unlock the creative spirits and genuine inquisitiveness of young people. These learners are drawn to Hemingway's zest for life, they are attracted by the astounding places he traveled and wrote about, and they are invited to the reading table by his economical style and then stunned by the complexity that lies beneath the surface. Lyons claims, "We feel, in all of Hemingway's tales of fishing, that he has special knowledge, true authority — but we never feel he is writing in ways that exclude those without such special knowledge" (xviii–xix). Many male students who have unfortunately been groomed by our society to shy away from reading are absorbed by Hemingway's books about fishing, hunting, and bullfighting. It is not uncommon to hear from students as they conclude essays that *The Old Man and the Sea* is the only book that has ever held their attention from start to finish. For some, reading it for my class is the only time they have ever finished a book, a realization that is disappointing on its surface but then wildly triumphant when fully considered.

Students respond favorably to Hemingway's unbridled philosophy about life and his ability to find so much pleasure in the world around him. When we study his fishing in the classroom, the stories and pictures allow my students to see Hemingway as a real human being who did extraordinary things — and then wrote books about them that I require students to read closely! In Hemingway's preface

to the 1953 second edition of Heilner's *Salt Water Fishing*, he asserted the sport is "for everyone. All branches of it are fun. There is no
game fish, from the gray snapper to the Mako shark, which does not
give pleasure to the angler" (viii). Farrington, who spent time fishing
with Hemingway, echoed this sentiment: "Ernest was as happy with
the catching of a five-pound fish as with catching a 400-pounder"
(*Fishing with Hemingway and Glassell* 17). Even after a very long
day on the ocean when he had to be exhausted, Farrington claimed,
Hemingway would sometimes still go bottom fishing at night just
like any amateur. Hendrickson points out when it became evident
in July 1935 that the *Pilar* required mechanical attention, Hemingway contentedly bottom-fished from shore in Bimini and worked on
Green Hills of Africa (327). Dos Passos recollected in his reflection
of traveling with Hemingway in *The Fisherman* magazine, "He had
his crotchety moments even then, but he was a barrel of monkeys to
be with. It was a period when life seemed enormously comical to all

of us. We carried things off with great fits of laughing" (Kemp, "The Fishing Life," 83). History comes alive when my students speculate about what all must have happened on that boat, and I am happy to let their imaginations run wild as they dream.

What a shame that a small contingent of influential critics have managed to have such a negative impact on Hemingway's position in the academy. Too many professors are avoiding the controversies that do not suit their politically correct designs, and I argue their evasion is at the expense of students who are hungry for literary works that speak to their imaginations. I was once one of those eager young students, and through the divine order of the universe, I first experienced Hemingway's world in that beach chair in 1994. His work instilled in me a lifelong love of reading, a passion for learning more, and an enhanced sense of adventure and curiosity.

According to Carlos Baker, Hemingway told his friends after the summer of 1935 that "the discovery of Bimini was a great event in his life: he liked it as well as any other place he had ever spent time in, and he was already eager to return to it [...] even before he left it" (352–53). Bimini, with its laid-back sensibility, its wonderfully welcoming islanders, its immaculate fishing grounds, and its perfectly secluded atmosphere, provided exactly what he needed at that juncture in his life. He wrote to Max Perkins on May 1, 1935, to say he could fly to Bimini lickety-split from Miami and yet it still felt like "the end of the world." The miraculous story of Hemingway at "the end of the world" birthed so many brilliant beginnings: a vibrant fishing economy for the island, the development of big-game fishing as a sport, an international organization to support and manage it, and the genesis of several pieces of incredibly important fiction and nonfiction from one of the 20th century's most significant writers — not bad for 197 days of fishing around a tiny little speck of salty land.

Ernest Hemingway and Carlos Gutiérrez discuss things
on board the *Pilar* in 1934.

A Chronology:
Important Dates and Events

1899

Ernest Miller Hemingway is born in Oak Park, Illinois, on July 21.

1901

Hemingway's father gives him his first fishing rod (before age 3).

1910

The young Hemingway makes his first visit to the ocean (Nantucket Island).

1920

Van Campen Heilner sets up his Bimini fishing camp.

1921

Hemingway marries Hadley Richardson. They honeymoon in Europe, where the author views huge game fish at a market.

1922

The Bimini Bay Rod and Gun Club opens. Construction began in 1920.

1925

Heilner catches two small blue marlin in Bimini.

Hemingway and Hadley meet Pauline Pfeiffer in Paris in March.

1926

A hurricane devastates Bimini and wipes out the Bimini Bay Rod and Gun Club.

1927

Hemingway divorces Hadley in March and marries Pauline in May.

Zane Grey's *Tales of Swordfish and Tuna* is released.

1928

Hemingway first visits Cuba on layover during a Spain trip. This is the same year he meets Gregorio Fuentes for the first time.

The author makes his inaugural visit to Key West.

1931

The Whitehead Street house in Key West is purchased by the Hemingways.

1932

Hemingway fishes for the first time in Cuba with Josie Russell aboard the *Anita*.

1933

Hemingway catches a marlin weighing 468 pounds, his first big game fish.

Michael and Helen Lerner visit Bimini for the first time. So do S. Kip Farrington, Jr., Lou Wasey, and Tommy Gifford.

February 28: Farrington catches the first blue marlin (155 pounds) on record in Bimini. The fish was the first of the species ever documented east of the Gulf Stream.

Helen Duncombe's Dower House opens.

The Lerners build the Anchorage.

1934

Hemingway purchases the *Pilar* in May.

Hemingway catches a 119.5-pound sailfish, setting an Atlantic record.

The author fishes during the month of August in Cuba with Charles M.
B. Cadwalader and Henry W. Fowler on an expedition for the Academy of
Natural Sciences.

The Dower House burns down on November 18.

1935

The Compleat Angler Hotel opens.

The terrible Labor Day Hurricane of 1935 strikes.

April 7

Hemingway first attempts to get to Bimini, shooting himself in both legs on
the way.

April 15

A slightly altered fishing party makes the Bimini trip successfully.

Hemingway meets Michael Lerner.

May 15

American Big Game Fishing is published.

Sometime in May, the author acquires a tommy gun from Bill Leeds and uses it
to spray the sharks that attack Mike Strater's 1,000-pound marlin.

May 21

Hemingway boats the first unmutilated tuna in Bimini. It weighed 381 pounds.

May 23

He lands the second unmutilated tuna, this one tipping the scales at
319 pounds.

May 26

Nathaniel Saunders witnesses Hemingway's dockside fight with Joseph Knapp,
commemorating the "Big Fat Slob" incident with his superb song.

June 22

Hemingway sets a North American record by catching a 786-pound
mako shark.

Hemingway needles himself for shooting both his legs in *Esquire*'s "On Being
Shot Again."

November: Hemingway is elected vice president of the Salt Water Anglers of
America.

Hemingway's purchase of the Bimini land is completed at the end of the year.

1936

The summer of 1936 is a very glamorous time for fishing in Bimini with people such as Tommy Shevlin, the Lerners, the Hemingways, the Farringtons, and author Marjorie Kinnan Rawlings in town.

The Spanish Civil War begins in July.

The Bahamas Marlin and Tuna Club is organized on November 23.

Hemingway meets Martha Gellhorn at Sloppy Joe's in Key West in December.

The Bimini Big Game Fishing Club is established by Neville Stuart.

1937

Hemingway spends 37 days in Bimini over several short trips. His fishing on the island is interrupted by his involvement with the Spanish Civil War.

Farrington's *Atlantic Game Fishing* is published.

Heilner's *Salt Water Fishing* is released.

1939

Hemingway goes to Cuba with Gellhorn.

The Spanish Civil War ends in April.

The IGFA forms at American Museum of Natural History in New York City on June 7.

World War II erupts in September, gripping the globe in turmoil.

1940

The author divorces second wife Pauline Pfeiffer in November and moves in with Gellhorn at the Finca Vigía in Cuba, first renting and then buying the property.

Hemingway marries Gellhorn in November.

1945

World War II ends in September.

The Hemingway-Gellhorn divorce is finalized in December.

1946

Mary Welsh marries Hemingway in March.

1948

The Lerner Marine Laboratory opens in Bimini.

1952

The Old Man and the Sea is published.

1953

The Pulitzer Prize is awarded to Hemingway for *The Old Man and the Sea*.

1954

Hemingway is awarded the Nobel Prize in Literature.

1961

Hemingway dies by suicide on July 2 in Ketchum, Idaho.

1970

Heilner dies in Madrid, Spain, on July 12.

Islands in the Stream is released posthumously, with *Esquire* publishing the "Bimini" excerpt in its October edition.

1972–1975

The Lerner Marine Laboratory closes.

1978

Mike Lerner dies on April 16 from cancer.

1983

Kip Farrington dies in New York State on February 7.

1998

The International Game Fish Association Hall of Fame inducts its first class of 29 anglers, including Hemingway, Heilner, Lerner, Farrington, Gifford, and Grey.

2006

The Compleat Angler is destroyed by fire on January 13. Owner Julian Brown is tragically killed in the accident.

The IGFA at sunset.

Acknowledgments

Special thanks are due to:

The John F. Kennedy Library Foundation for awarding me the Ernest Hemingway Research Grant. The funds allowed my dream of visiting the Hemingway Collection at the Kennedy Presidential Library in Boston to become a reality, and the insight I gained there was integral to this project.

The Selection Committee for the 17th biennial international Hemingway Society Conference in Oak Park, Illinois, July 17–22, 2016. The opportunity to present my research to the foremost Hemingway critics in the world was invaluable.

Sheriffa Robinson, Mike Myatt, Adrian Gray, and Jason Schratwieser at the International Game Fish Association headquarters in Dania Beach, Florida. Sheriffa devoted a whole day to guiding me through the E. K. Harry Library of Fishes collection and spent hours scanning dozens of vintage photographs that appear in this book. Adrian's outstanding photographs of the IGFA building are breathtaking. I am proud to be an IGFA member and to know you all.

Stephen Plotkin and all the staff members at the Ernest Hemingway Research Room at the JFK Library. **Laurie Austin** and **Maryrose Grossman** in the audiovisual archives at the library were also extraordinarily helpful.

Mai Reitmeyer, Research Services Librarian at the American Museum of Natural History in New York, for her tremendous assistance with several documents from the AMNH collection, including scans of letters, cables, and newspaper clippings.

The Rare Books and Special Collections Department at the Princeton University Library for its help with several letters from the archives of Charles Scribner's Sons.

The Special Collections staff at the University of Miami Library for their insight about the Erl Roman papers.

Lara Little, the director of the Gustavus Adolphus Library at Pfeiffer University. Hug a librarian today — especially the one who handles all of your interlibrary loans.

Molly Battles, Public Relations Manager for *Popular Science*, *Field & Stream*, and *Outdoor Life*, and **Jean McKenna**, Managing Editor for *Field & Stream* and *Outdoor Life*. They scoured their archives for pictures and answered more than one question along the way.

Hilary Hemingway, for the candid personal interview. I am grateful for your willingness to share details about your family.

Dr. Kirk Curnutt, a professor of English at Troy University Montgomery and a longtime member of the Hemingway Society board. Kirk answered several very complicated questions about fair use and offered great advice.

Sir Michael Checkley, the director of the Bimini Museum. He responded to many e-mail questions about Bimini history that arose after I left the island, and he offered various resources to help sort through information from contradictory texts.

The people of Bimini, including **Natty Saunders, Ansil Saunders, Thomas Saunders, Ashley Saunders, Joemond Jones**, **Cleveland Francis,** and many others. Thank you for welcoming a complete stranger into your homes and taking the time to answer her seemingly endless list of questions. Thanks as well to the wonderful staff at the Hilton World Resorts Bimini.

Dr. Boyd Davis, Dr. Tony Jackson, and **Dr. Gail McDonald,** for constantly challenging me in and out of the graduate classroom. Your tireless mentoring demonstrated your belief in me, which made it possible for me to believe in my ability to tackle this project.

Navigating the darker corners of Hemingway's life was a challenge. Thank you to **Rev. Dana McKim, Rev. Sherri Barnes, Claudette Scott,** and **Paula Morris** for helping me guard my steps and for always guiding me toward The Light.

My brother **Troy Williams**, for being my most enthusiastic supporter. Your genuine excitement for my books means more than you will ever know.

Joe and Beth Yarbrough, for paying a lot of college tuition to pull me through the Ph.D. that prepared me to write this book. Beth is also responsible for the lovely Bimini map that appears in Chapter I.

And last but certainly not least, my dear husband **Chris Oliphant**. He is the coconut bowling champion of South Bimini and the love of my life.

Works Cited

"100 Year Old Nathaniel 'Piccolo Pete' Saunders of Bimini Honoured!" *Bahama Press*. 19 November 2014. Web. 21 May 2016.

Albury, Paul. *The Story of the Bahamas*. London and Oxford: Macmillan Education Ltd, 1975. Print.

"The American Museum of Natural History Seventy-Fifth Annual Report for the Year 1943." *New York: American Museum of Natural History*, 1 May 1944. Web. 14 July 2016.

"Atlantis." *The History Channel Online*. 2015. Web. 13 September 2015.

"The Bahamas." *The Bahamas Online*. 2016. Web. 21 January 2016.

"The Bahamas Pays Tribute to Dr. Martin Luther King, Jr. *Caricom Caribbean Community*. 19 January 2015. Web. 31 May 2016.

Baker, Carlos. *Ernest Hemingway: A Life Story*. New York: Bantam, 1969. Print.

Barratt, Peter. *Bahama Saga: The Epic Story of the Bahama Islands*. Bloomington: AuthorHouse, 2008. Print.

Beckles, Hilary, and Verene A. Shepherd. *Liberties Lost: Caribbean Indigenous Societies and Slave Systems*. Cambridge: Cambridge University Press, 2004. Print.

Bell, John. "Bimini Beckons." *GAFF Magazine* July/August 2011: 36–40. Web. 3 June 2016.

Belasco, Susan, and Linck Johnson, eds. *The Bedford Anthology of American Literature Volume One: Beginnings to 1865*. Boston and New York: Bedford/St. Martin's, 2008. Print.

Benchley, Peter. "The Scene / Cat Cay: Rebirth for a Snooty Eden." *Life* 23 May 1969: 26–28. Print.

Bennett, Steve. "Uncommon Attraction: The Spooky Wreck of the SS *Sapona*." *Uncommon Caribbean*. 23 January 2013. Web. 23 January 2016.

"Big Game Fish Bimini Bahamas." *Bimini Bahamas Online*. 2016. Web. 22 June 2016.

"Big Game Sport Fishing." *Bimini's Heritage Centre/Bimini Museum Online*. 2015. Web. 7 September 2015.

Bignami, Louis. "Heavyweight Fishing Records." *Fine Fishing*. 2015. Web. 17 June 2016.

"Bimini's Academic Program." *The Hemingway Newsletter* 39 (January 2000): 2. Web. 14 July 2016.

"Bimini Compleat Angler Burned Down." *The Hull Truth Boating and Fishing Forum*. 14 January 2006. Web. 31 May 2016.

"Bimini Is The Sport Fishing Capital of the World." *The Out Islands of the Bahamas Online*. 2014. Web. 22 June 2016.

"British Bimini and American Prohibition 1920-1933." *Bimini's Heritage Centre/Bimini Museum Online*. 2015. Web. 10 June 2016.

Bryan, Susannah. "Fishing Hall of Fame, Museum to bid farewell to Dania Beach." *Sun Sentinel Online* 20 March 2015. Web. 22 August 2015.

Brykczynski, Terry, David Reuther, and John Thorn, eds. *The Armchair Angler*. New York: Charles Scribner's Sons, 1986. Print.

Buffett, Jimmy. "Margaritaville." *Changes in Latitudes, Changes in Attitudes*. ABC, 1977. CD.

———. *Tales from Margaritaville*. San Diego: Harcourt Brace Jovanovich, 1989. Print.

Buffett, Jimmy, and Roger Guth. "Tides." *Songs from St. Somewhere*. Mailboat, 2013. MP3.

Butler, Lindley S. *Pirates, Privateers, and Rebel Raiders of the Carolina Coast*. Chapel Hill: The University of North Carolina Press, 2000. Print.

Cardoni, Alex. "Twenty Hours on Bimini." January 1996. Print.

Castro, Fidel, and Ignacio Ramonet. *Fidel Castro: My Life*. New York: Scribner, 2006. Print.

"The Centurion." *Bimini Times Newspaper Online* 2015 Bimini Edition Issue 1: 4. Web.

Chamberlin, Brewster. *The Hemingway Log: A Chronology of His Life and Times*. Lawrence: University Press of Kansas, 2015. Print.

Checkley, Sir Michael. Personal interview. 25 January 2016, 27 January 2016, and 25 April 2016.

Cole, Richard. "Drug Smugglers Control South Bimini, Say Officials." *Ocala Star-Banner* 11 May 1989: 5B. Web. 21 May 2016.

Craton, Michael. *A History of the Bahamas*. 3rd ed. Ontario: San Salvador Press, 1986. Print.

Craton, Michael, and Gail Saunders. *Islanders in the Stream: A History of the Bahamian People. Volume One: From Aboriginal Times to the End of Slavery*. Athens and London: The University of Georgia Press, 1992. Print.

————. *Islanders in the Stream: A History of the Bahamian People. Volume Two: From the Ending of Slavery to the Twenty-First Century*. Athens and London: The University of Georgia Press, 1998. Print.

Currington, Billy, Scotty Emerick, and John Scott Sherrill. "Bad Day of Fishin'." *Enjoy Yourself*. Mercury Nashville, 2010. MP3.

David, Ebbie. Personal interview. 8 January 2016.

Davis, Craig. "The Second Sight of Bimini's Bonefish Willie." *Sun Sentinel Online* 22 September 1986. Web. 22 June 2016.

Davis, Sandra. "Bimini Museum & Heritage Center." *Bahamas Bliss: Bimini*. 23 September 2013. Web. 11 September 2016.

———— "Bimini Rod and Gun Club Ruins." *Bahamas Bliss: Bimini*. 23 September 2013. Web. 4 June 2016.

————. "Buffett in Bimini." *Bahamas Bliss: Bimini*. 23 September 2013. Web. 31 May 2016.

————. "Marlin Cottage." *Bahamas Bliss: Bimini*. 23 September 2013. Web. 1 June 2016.

Day, Jane. "Bimini, Bahamas: Hemingway's Island in the Stream." *South Florida History Magazine* Fall 1989: 5–9, 24. Print.

DeFalco, Joseph M. "'Bimini' and the Subject of Hemingway's *Islands in the Stream*." *Topic* 31 (1977): 41–51. Print.

"Derek Walcott Keynote Speaker at Bimini International Meeting." *The Hemingway Newsletter* 38 (June 1999): 1–2. Print.

DiPano, Robert. "Bimini's New Cruise Ship Pier Opens." *Caribbean Journal*. 19 September 2014. Web. 7 September 2015.

Dos Passos, John. "Old Hem Was a Sport." *Sports Illustrated* 29 June 1964: 58–67. Print.

Doty, G. H. "Bimini Blues: Part One." *Motor Boating: The Yachtsmen's Magazine* (November 1937): 22–25, 80. Web.

———. "Bimini Blues: Part Two." *Motor Boating: The Yachtsmen's Magazine* (December 1937): 24–27. Web.

———. "Bimini Blues: Part Three." *Motor Boating: The Yachtsmen's Magazine* (January 1938): 50–53, 218. Web.

Eilperin, Juliet. "Bahamas Bans Commercial Shark Fishing." *Project Aware*. 5 July 2011. Web. 3 June 2016.

Ernest Hemingway Selected Letters 1917–1961. Ed. Carlos Baker. New York: Charles Scribner's Sons, 1981. Print.

Farrington, S. Kip, Jr. *Atlantic Game Fishing*. New York: Kennedy Brothers, Inc., 1937. Print.

———. "Ever Hook a Blue Torpedo?" *The Rotarian* (May 1936): 11–13, 50–51. Print.

———. "Fishing at Bimini." *American Big Game Fishing*. Ed. Eugene V. Connett III. Lanham and New York: Derrydale Press, 1993. Print. 109–127.

———. *Fishing with Hemingway and Glassell*. New York: David McKay Company, 1971. Print.

"Fast Facts: Bimini." *Frommer's Online*. FrommerMediaLLC, 2016. Web. 21 May 2016.

"Fire razes Hemingway island haunt." *BBC News*. 14 January 2006. Web. 25 July 2015.

"Four New IGFA Records Set in Bimini." *Guy Harvey Outpost Online*. 22 November 2010. Web. 22 June 2016.

Francis, Cleveland. Personal interview. 7 January 2016.

Frey, David. "A Hemingway Returns to Bimini." *Papa's Planet: An Ernest Exploration of the Places Hemingway Lived and Loved*. 26 January 2013. Web. 25 July 2015.

Fuentes, Norberto. *Hemingway in Cuba*. Secaucus: Lyle Stuart, 1984. Print.

Gajdusek, Robert E. "The Hemingway of Cuba and Bimini and His Later Relationship to Nature." *North Dakota Quarterly* 68.2-3 (Spring/Summer 2001): 91–108. Print.

————. "'New' Bimini Museum Opens at Compleat Angler Inn; First Convocation Held." *The Hemingway Newsletter* 20 (June 1995): 2. Web.

German, Norman. "Rehabilitating Hemingway." *Salt Water Sportsman* 66.1 (January 2005). Web. 11 September 2015.

Gingrich, Arnold. *The Well-Tempered Angler*. New York: Alfred A. Knopf, 1966. Print.

Goadby, Peter. *Saltwater Gamefishing Offshore and Onshore*. Camden: International Marine/TAB Books, 1992. Print.

Gordon, Sarah. "The Battle for Bimini: Hemingway's Bahamas Paradise under Threat as Locals Row over Plans to Bring in 500,000 Tourists a Year." *Daily Mail*. 6 July 2014. Web. 27 January 2015.

Grey, Zane. *Tales of Swordfish and Tuna*. New York and London: Harper & Brothers Publishers, 1927. Print.

"Guy Harvey's Bimini Big Game Club Re-Opens Historic Gulfstream Room." *Guy Harvey Outpost Online*. 29 March 2011. Web. 22 June 2016.

Hawkins, Ruth A. *Unbelievable Happiness and Final Sorrow: The Hemingway-Pfeiffer Marriage*. Fayetteville: University of Arkansas Press, 2012. Print.

Heilner, Van Campen. *Salt Water Fishing*. 2nd edition revised. New York: Alfred A. Knopf, 1953. Print.

Hemingway and the Mechanism of Fame: Statements, Public Letters, Introductions, Forewords, Prefaces, Blurbs, Reviews, and Endorsements. Ed Matthew J. Bruccoli. Columbia: University of South Carolina Press, 2006. Print.

Hemingway, Ernest. "a.d. Southern Style: A Key West Letter." *Esquire* (May 1935): 25, 156. Print.

————. "Bimini." *Esquire* (October 1970): 121–137, 190–202. Print.

————. *Hemingway on Fishing*. Ed. Nick Lyons. New York: The Lyons Press, 2000. Print.

————. "The Great Blue River." *Holiday* (July 1949): 60–63 and 95. Print.

————. "Hemingway on Mutilated Fish." *Outdoor Life* 77 (June 1936): 70–72. Print.

————. "He Who Gets Slap Happy: A Bimini Letter." *Esquire* (August 1935): 19, 182. Print.

————. *Islands in the Stream*. New York: Charles Scribner's Sons, 1970. Print.

————. "Marlin off Cuba." *American Big Game Fishing*. Ed. Eugene V. Connett III. Lanham and New York: Derrydale Press, 1993. Print. 55–81.

————. *The Old Man and the Sea*. New York: Simon & Schuster, 1995. Print.

————. "On Being Shot Again." *Esquire* (June 1935): 25, 156–57. Print.

————. "Preface." *Salt Water Fishing*. 2nd edition revised. New York: Alfred A. Knopf, 1953. Print.

————. "The President Vanquishes: A Bimini Letter." *Esquire* (July 1935): 23, 167. Print.

"Hemingway Fishing Tournament." *Hemingway Cuba Online*. 2015. Web. 22 June 2016.

Hemingway, Gregory. *Papa: A Personal Memoir*. Boston: Houghton Mifflin, 1976. Print.

Hemingway, Hilary, and Carlene Brennen. *Hemingway in Cuba*. New York: Rugged Land, 2003. Print.

Hemingway, Hilary. Personal interview. 10 June 2016.

Hemingway, Jack. *Misadventures of a Fly Fisherman: My Life with and without Papa*. Dallas: Taylor Publishing Company, 1986. Print.

Hemingway, John Patrick. "Hemingway: A Love Affair with Bimini." *Sport Fishing Magazine* 2 April 2013. Web. 25 July 2015.

Hemmingson, Michael. "*Esquire*'s Failure with Hemingway's 'Bimini.'" *The Hemingway Review* 29.1 (Fall 2009): 140–144. Print.

Hendrickson, Paul. *Hemingway's Boat: Everything He Loved in Life, and Lost*. New York: Vintage Books, 2011. Print.

Hennesey, Hal. "Exploring the Bahamas: Part One." *Boating* (November 1967): 20–23, 70–73. Print.

————. "Exploring the Bahamas: Part Two." *Boating* (December 1967): 39–42, 80–82. Print.

Hotchner, A. E. *Hemingway in Love: His Own Story*. New York: St. Martin's Press, 2015. Print.

Houk, Walter. "Notes on 'Hemingway in Bimini.'" *North Dakota Quarterly* 65.3 (1998): 219–20. Print.

————. "A Sailor Looks at Hemingway's *Islands*." *North Dakota Quarterly* 73.1–2 (Winter/Spring 2006): 7–74. Print.

"How Fast is the Gulf Stream?" *National Oceanic and Atmospheric Administration Online*. 24 March 2015. Web. 8 July 2016.

Hudson, Sam. "Bahamas Blue Marlin Record Broken." *Florida Sportsman Online.* 6 July 2011. Web. 22 June 2016.

Hulse, Jerry. "Some Insist It Was Here that Nobel Prize-Winning Papa Hemingway Got the Inspiration for His Novel about '*The Old Man and the Sea.*' Bimini." *Los Angeles Times* 5 May 1985. Web. 25 July 2015.

Hunt, Lynn Bogue. "Sailfish." *American Big Game Fishing.* Ed. Eugene V Connett III. Lanham and New York: Derrydale Press, 1993. Print. 1–53.

"IGFA History: Francesca LaMonte." *International Game Fish Association Online.* 2015. Web. 17 June 2016.

"IGFA World Records." *IGFA Online.* 2016. Web. 22 June 2016.

"International Game Fish Association Hall of Fame Inductees." *IGFA Online.* 2015. Web. 13 June 2016.

Johnson, et al. "Reflections on Bimini and the Compleat Angler." *North Dakota Quarterly* 73.1–2 (Winter/Spring 2006): 245–256. Print.

Jones, Joemond. Personal interview. 8 January 2016.

Junkins, Donald. "Bimini by the Sea." *North Dakota Quarterly* 73.1–2 (Winter/ Spring 2006): 252–255. Print.

Kelly, Doug. *Florida's Fishing Legends and Pioneers.* Gainesville: University Press of Florida, 2011. Print.

Kemp, Tom. "The Fishing Life of Ernest Hemingway: The Great Author-Fisherman as Seen by a Reporter, by the Camera, and by His Friends John Dos Passos, Waldo Peirce, Taylor Williams." *The Fisherman* 9.1 (January 1958): 35–41, 78–86. Print.

———. "From the Two-Hearted to Havana: The Fishing Times of a Great Author." *The Fisherman* 9.1 (January 1958): 35–41, 78–86. Print.

Kresge, Dave. *Bimini Cruising Guide.* IGFA Archives. 2003. Print.

Lambert, Marjie. "Resorts World ending cruises to Bimini." *Miami Herald* 8 January 2016. *Miami Herald Online.* Web. 19 January 2016.

LaMonte, Francesca. "Lerner-Bimini Expedition (1937): Report to the Director," About August 16, 1937. Central Archives, 1216; American Museum of Natural History Library.

Lawrence, H. Lea. *Prowling Papa's Waters: A Hemingway Odyssey.* Atlanta: Longstreet Press, 1992. Print.

Lee, Robert E. *Blackbeard the Pirate: A Reappraisal of His Life and Times.* Winston-Salem: John F. Blair, 1998. Print.

"Lee Wulff – IGFA Fishing Hall of Fame." Online video clip. YouTube, 24 August 2012. Web. 17 January 2016.

Lyons, Nick, ed. "Introduction." *Hemingway on Fishing*. By Ernest Hemingway. New York: The Lyons Press, 2000. Print. xvii–xxix.

Major, H. W. "The Human Side of the Fish." *Motor Boating Magazine* May 1934: 44–45, 106–108. Web.

Martin, Lawrence H. "Ernest Hemingway, Gulf Stream Marine Scientist: The 1934–35 Academy of Natural Sciences Correspondence." *The Hemingway Review* 20.2 (Spring 2001): 5–15. Print.

McDonald, Tim. "On Bimini, Bell Tolls for Hemingway's Legend." *Los Angeles Times* 1 October 2000. Web. 15 September 2016.

———. "Tiny Island, Made Large by Hemingway." *Los Angeles Times* 1 October 2000. Web. 6 September 2015.

McIver, Stuart B. *Hemingway's Key West*. 2nd Ed. Sarasota: Pineapple Press, 2002. Print.

———. "The Reel Hemingway." *Sun Sentinel Online* 18 July 1999. Web. 7 September 2015.

McNeil, Jeremy. Personal interview. 8 January 2016.

Meyers, Jeffrey. *Hemingway: A Biography*. New York: Harper & Row, 1985. Print.

Miller, Linda Patterson. "The Matrix of Hemingway's *Pilar* Log, 1934–1935." *The North Dakota Quarterly* 64.3 (Summer 1997): 105–23. Print.

Mitchell, Margaret. *Gone with the Wind*. New York: Avon Books, 1973. Print.

Oliphant, Ashley. "The Keys are the Key: A Defense of the Narrative Structure of Hemingway's *To Have and Have Not*." 11th Biennial International Ernest Hemingway Society Conference. Key West, Florida, June 2004.

Oliver, Charles M. *Ernest Hemingway A to Z: The Essential Reference to the Life and Work*. New York: Checkmark Books, 1999. Print.

Ott, Mark P. *A Sea of Change: Ernest Hemingway and the Gulf Stream*. Kent: Kent State University Press, 2008. Print.

Peters, Thelma. "Blockade-Running in the Bahamas During the Civil War." Historical Association of Southern Florida Meeting. 5 May 1943. Print.

"Pirate Den: New Providence." *The Way of the Pirates Online*. 2015. Web. 14 September 2015.

Plato Unmasked: The Dialogues Made New. Trans. Keith Quincy. Spokane: Eastern Washington University Press, 2003. Print.

Reiger, George. *Profiles in Saltwater Angling: A History of the Sport – Its People and Places, Tackle and Techniques*. Englewood Cliffs: Prentice Hall, 1973. Print.

Reynolds, Michael. *Hemingway in the 1930s*. New York and London: W. W. Norton & Company, 1997. Print.

Rivkin, Mike. *Big-Game Fishing Headquarters: A History of the IGFA*. Dania Beach: IGFA Press, 2005. Print.

Rogers, Mark. "Where the Sun Rises: Exploring Ernest Hemingway's Caribbean." *USA Today* 25 June 2015. Web. 14 July 2016.

Roman, Erl. "Fishing." *Motor Boating* 61.5 (May 1938): 19–20. Print.

Rusk, Howard A. "Bimini Has Great Marine Laboratory." *The Day* 25 April 1969: 24. Print.

"Salt Water Anglers of America Mission Statement," February 1935. Central Archives, 1267; American Museum of Natural History Library.

Saunders, Ansil. Personal interview. 9 January 2016.

Saunders, Ashley B. *History of Bimini Volume 1*. Alice Town: New World Press, 1989. Print.

Saunders, Ashley B. *History of Bimini Volume 2*. Alice Town: New World Press, 1992. Print.

————. Personal interview. 7 January 2016.

Saunders, Nathaniel. "Big Fat Slob." Bimini Nights. *Victory Records*, 2002. MP3.

————. Personal interview. 8 January 2016.

Saunders, Thomas. Personal interview. 7 January 2016.

Schratwieser, Jason. Personal interview. 24 August 2015 and 8 January 2016.

Skipp, Francis E. "Metempsychosis in the Stream, or What Happens in 'Bimini'?" *Fitzgerald/Hemingway Annual*: 1974. 137–143. Print.

Smith, Larry. "Hemingway Legacy Brings Bimini into Focus." *Bahama Pundit: A Selection of Weekly Articles by Top Bahamian Commentators*. 6 February 2013. Web. 23 July 2015.

Stoneback, H. R. "The View from the Verandah: The Hemingway Room at the Compleat Angler." *North Dakota Quarterly* 73.1–2 (Winter/Spring 2006): 246–50. Print.

Tessitore, John. *The Hunt and the Feast: A Life of Ernest Hemingway*. New York: Franklin Watts, 1996. Print.

"Thomas M. Gifford." *IGFA Hall of Fame*. 2015. Web. 4 June 2016.

Thomas, Robert McG., Jr. "S. Kip Farrington Jr. Is Dead; Was a Sportsman and Writer." *The New York Times* 8 February 1983. Web. 7 September 2015.

Thornton, Dade W. "A History of Big Game Fishing in the Bahamas." *International Game Fish Association Library*. Print.

"Timeline: Bahamas – A Chronology of Key Events." *BBC News*. 2015. Web. 13 September 2015.

Trogdon, Robert W. *Ernest Hemingway: A Literary Reference*. New York: Carroll & Graf, 1999. Print.

Trullinger, Ray. "New Big Fish Club Is Organized, But It's Awfully Hard to Crash." *N.Y.C. World-Telegram* 23 November 1936. Print.

Tryckare, Tre, and E. Cagner. *The Lore of Sportfishing*. New York: Crown Publishers, 1976. Print.

"Van Campen Heilner." *IGFA Hall of Fame Online*. 2015. Web. 6 June 2016.

Volz, Schuyler. "AMNH Research Stations: Past and Present." *American Museum of Natural History Hidden Collections: Stories from the Archive*. American Museum of Natural History, 20 April 2012. Web. 25 August 2015.

Waitzkin, Bonnie. "Fishing the Caribbean: From Walker's Cay to the West Indies the Caribbean is an Angler's Paradise." *Motor Boating & Sailing* 156.5 (November 1985): 68–72. Print.

Watson, William Braasch. "Hemingway in Bimini: An Introduction." *North Dakota Quarterly* 63.3 (Summer 1996): 130–44. Print.

"Wrecking 1840–1919." *Bimini's Heritage Centre Bimini Bahamas Online*. 2016. Web. 23 January 2016.

Wylie, Philip. "Big Fish and High Seas." *Esquire* (November 1952): 63–67. Print.

———. *The Lerner Marine Laboratory at Bimini Bahamas*. New York: American Museum of Natural History, 1960. Web.

"Zane Grey." *IGFA Hall of Fame*. 2015. Web. 8 July 2016.

Letters Cited

Preface

Hemingway to Jane Mason, June 3, 1935, John F. Kennedy Library, Hemingway Collection.

Chapter I

Hemingway to Sara Murphy, July 10, 1935, Hendrickson 328.

Chapter II

Hemingway to Jane Mason, June 3, 1935, John F. Kennedy Library, Hemingway Collection.

Zane Grey to Dr. William K. Gregory, June 11, 1926. Central Archives, 1209; American Museum of Natural History Library.

Vice-Director of the AMNH (likely W. M. Faunce) to Orton G. Dale, Jr., February 11, 1935. Central Archives, 1267; American Museum of Natural History Library.

Hemingway to Charles M. B. Cadwalader, September 6, 1934, John F. Kennedy Library, Hemingway Collection.

Hemingway to Cadwalader, April 2, 1934, John F. Kennedy Library, Hemingway Collection.

Hemingway to Cadwalader, April 9, 1934, John F. Kennedy Library, Hemingway Collection.

Hemingway to Henry W. Fowler, July 9, 1934, John F. Kennedy Library, Hemingway Collection.

Hemingway to Fowler, October 1, 1934, John F. Kennedy Library, Hemingway Collection.

Hemingway to Mike Strater, July 1933, Hendrickson 292.

Zane Grey to Hemingway, March 19, 1935, John F. Kennedy Library, Hemingway Collection.

S. Kip Farrington, Jr. to Erl Roman, June 20, 1935, International Game Fish Association Library.

Chapter III

Michael Lerner to Hemingway, December 1935, John F. Kennedy Library, Hemingway Collection.

Hemingway to Baron Bror von Blixen, May 22, 1935, John F. Kennedy Library, Hemingway Collection.

Hemingway to Mason, June 3, 1935, John F. Kennedy Library, Hemingway Collection.

Hemingway to Lerner, May 19, 1936, John F. Kennedy Library, Hemingway Collection.

Lerner to Hemingway, December 4, 1935, John F. Kennedy Library, Hemingway Collection.

Hemingway to Lerner, March 23, 1936, John F. Kennedy Library, Hemingway Collection.

Lerner to Hemingway, April 2, 1937, John F. Kennedy Library, Hemingway Collection.

Hemingway to Max Perkins, July 30, 1935, Princeton University Library, Charles Scribner's Sons Collection.

Hemingway to Murphy, July 1935, Day 7.

Hemingway to Waldo Peirce, July 27, 1937, John F. Kennedy Library, Hemingway Collection.

Chapter IV

Vice-Director of the AMNH (likely W. M. Faunce) to Orton G. Dale, Jr., February 11, 1935. Central Archives, 1267; American Museum of Natural History Library.

Van Campen Heilner to Mr. W. M. Faunce, February 13, 1935. Central Archives, 1267; American Museum of Natural History Library.

Mrs. Oliver C. Grinnell to Hemingway, August 29, 1935, John F. Kennedy Library, Hemingway Collection.

Roman to Hemingway, August 29, 1935, John F. Kennedy Library, Hemingway Collection.

Hemingway to Grinnell, September 1935, John F. Kennedy Library, Hemingway Collection.

Lerner to Hemingway, May 7, 1936, John F. Kennedy Library, Hemingway Collection.

Hemingway to Lerner, June 1936 Pilot Boat Day, John F. Kennedy Library, Hemingway Collection.

Kip Farrington to Hemingway, December 4, 1936, John F. Kennedy Library, Hemingway Collection.

Lerner to Hemingway, August 19, 1937, John F. Kennedy Library, Hemingway Collection.

Lerner to Hemingway, January 4, 1938, John F. Kennedy Library, Hemingway Collection.

Hemingway to Lerner, March 4, 1937, John F. Kennedy Library, Hemingway Collection.

Lerner to Hemingway, April 2, 1937, John F. Kennedy Library, Hemingway Collection.

John T. Nichols to Roy C. Andrews, March 25, 1940. Central Archives, 1290.4; American Museum of Natural History Library.

Lerner to Hemingway, July 13, 1943, John F. Kennedy Library, Hemingway Collection.

Hemingway to Lerner, August 2, 1943, John F. Kennedy Library, Hemingway Collection.

Lerner to Hemingway, May 22, 1937, John F. Kennedy Library, Hemingway Collection.

Hemingway to Lerner, March 1936, McIver 124.

Chapter V

Hemingway to Peirce, July 27, 1937, John F. Kennedy Library, Hemingway Collection.

Helen Lerner to Pauline and Ernest Hemingway, February 3, 1937, John F. Kennedy Library, Hemingway Collection.

Hemingway to Lerner, March 4, 1937, John F. Kennedy Library, Hemingway Collection.

Hemingway to Lerner, August 18, 1935, John F. Kennedy Library, Hemingway Collection.

Hemingway to Lerner, July 18, 1938, John F. Kennedy Library, Hemingway Collection.

Hemingway to Tommy Shevlin, April 4, 1939, John F. Kennedy Library, Hemingway Collection.

Hemingway to Perkins, July 1935, Princeton University Library.

Helen Lerner to Pauline and Ernest Hemingway, May 19, 1936, John F. Kennedy Library, Hemingway Collection.

Mike Lerner to Hemingway, June 5, 1936, John F. Kennedy Library, Hemingway Collection.

Hemingway to Lerner, December 15, 1935, John F. Kennedy Library, Hemingway Collection.

Mary Hemingway to Bill Seward, August 22, 1958, John F. Kennedy Library, Hemingway Collection.

Chapter VI

Lerner to Hemingway, November 19, 1936, John F. Kennedy Library, Hemingway Collection.

Lerner to Hemingway, October 30, 1943, John F. Kennedy Library, Hemingway Collection.

Lerner to Hemingway, June 21, 1950, John F. Kennedy Library, Hemingway Collection.

Lerner to Hemingway, May 22, 1937, John F. Kennedy Library, Hemingway Collection.

Hemingway to Lerner, December 3, 1935, John F. Kennedy Library, Hemingway Collection.

Lerner to Hemingway, December 12, 1935, John F. Kennedy Library, Hemingway Collection.

Lerner to Hemingway, April 7, 1936, John F. Kennedy Library, Hemingway Collection.

Hemingway to Lerner, December 15, 1935, John F. Kennedy Library, Hemingway Collection.

Lerner to Hemingway, December 20, 1935, John F. Kennedy Library, Hemingway Collection.

Hemingway to Lerner, March 23, 1936, John F. Kennedy Library, Hemingway Collection.

Lerner to Hemingway, June 7, 1937, John F. Kennedy Library, Hemingway Collection.

Lerner to Hemingway, July 30, 1937, John F. Kennedy Library, Hemingway Collection.

Hemingway to Lerner, June 20, 1943, John F. Kennedy Library, Hemingway Collection.

Lerner to Hemingway, June 21, 1943, John F. Kennedy Library, Hemingway Collection.

Lerner to Hemingway, June 22, 1943, John F. Kennedy Library, Hemingway Collection.

Hemingway to Lerner, June 30, 1943, John F. Kennedy Library, Hemingway Collection.

Lerner to Hemingway, July 13, 1943, John F. Kennedy Library, Hemingway Collection.

Heilner to Francesca LaMonte, March 17, 1943. Central Archives, 1216; American Museum of Natural History Library.

LaMonte to Hemingway, March 18, 1943. Central Archives, 1216; American Museum of Natural History Library.

Hemingway to LaMonte, March 24, 1943. Central Archives, 1216; American Museum of Natural History Library.

Heilner to LaMonte, March 24, 1943. Central Archives, 1216; American Museum of Natural History Library.

Albert Eide Parr to Hemingway, March 29, 1943. Central Archives, 1216; American Museum of Natural History Library.

LaMonte internal memo to Addie Hill Summerson, About March 24, 1943. Central Archives, 1216; American Museum of Natural History Library.

Van Campen Heilner, August 24, 1943, John F. Kennedy Library, Hemingway Collection.

Hemingway to Heilner, September 6, 1943, John F. Kennedy Library, Hemingway Collection.

Hemingway to Lerner, October 18, 1943, John F. Kennedy Library, Hemingway Collection.

Lerner to Hemingway, October 23, 1943 (likely), John F. Kennedy Library, Hemingway Collection.

Lerner to Hemingway, January 4, 1944, John F. Kennedy Library, Hemingway Collection.

Hemingway to Mike and Helen Lerner, December 22, 1945, John F. Kennedy Library, Hemingway Collection.

Hemingway to Lerner, October 23, 1949, John F. Kennedy Library, Hemingway Collection.

Lerner to Hemingway, After October 23, 1949, John F. Kennedy Library, Hemingway Collection.

Lerner to Hemingway, June 21, 1950, John F. Kennedy Library, Hemingway Collection.

Lerner to Hemingway, August 22, 1950, John F. Kennedy Library, Hemingway Collection.

Hemingway to Arthur Gray, February 26, 1951. 1222.6; American Museum of Natural History Library.

Lerner to Hemingway, February 6, 1952, John F. Kennedy Library, Hemingway Collection.

Hemingway to Lerner, August 1959, John F. Kennedy Library, Hemingway Collection.

Afterword

Hemingway to Perkins, May 1, 1935, Princeton University Library.

Photo Credits

Photographs are by the author except for the following:

p. 14 IGFA Collection. Donated by Carol Chance

p. 16 IGFA Mike Lerner Collection

p. 20 Beth Yarbrough Design

p. 23 Public Domain

p. 33 Erl Roman Photograph / IGFA Collection

p. 40 *Field & Stream* Collection

p. 44 IGFA Collection

p. 45 IGFA Collection

p. 46 Erl Roman Photograph / IGFA Collection

p. 48 IGFA Mike Lerner Collection

p. 50 IGFA Mike Lerner Collection

p. 52 IGFA Collection

p. 56 John F. Kennedy Presidential Library Hemingway Collection

p. 58 Erl Roman Photograph / IGFA Joe Brooks Collection

p. 63 IGFA Collection

p. 65 John F. Kennedy Presidential Library Hemingway Collection

p. 68 IGFA Mike Lerner Collection

p. 70 IGFA Collection, Reprinted with permission from the IGFA

p. 75 IGFA Erl Roman Collection

p. 76 IGFA Collection / Donated by Carol Chance

p. 80 IGFA Joe Brooks Collection

p. 82 IGFA Mike Lerner Collection

p. 83 John F. Kennedy Presidential Library Hemingway Collection

p. 84 IGFA Mike Lerner Collection

p. 86 IGFA Mike Lerner Collection

p. 88 IGFA Collection

p. 89 Dade W. Thornton Photograph / IGFA George Reiger Collection

p. 91 *Field & Stream* Collection

p. 92 IGFA Mike Lerner Collection

p. 98 John F. Kennedy Presidential Library Hemingway Collection

p. 101 IGFA Collection

p. 102 IGFA Mike Lerner Collection

p. 106 IGFA Collection

p. 109 IGFA Collection

p. 114 Reprinted with permission from the AMNH Library

p. 122 Adrian Gray sportfishimages.com Photograph

p. 125 Adrian Gray sportfishimages.com Photograph

p. 133 IGFA Collection

p. 137 IGFA Collection

p. 138 IGFA Collection

p. 140 IGFA Joe Brooks Collection

p. 148 IGFA Collection

p. 154 IGFA Mike Lerner Collection

p. 158 IGFA Mike Lerner Collection

p. 178 IGFA Erl Roman Collection

p. 179 Reprinted courtesy of the American Museum of Natural History Library

p. 182 IGFA Mike Lerner Collection

p. 186 IGFA Mike Lerner Collection

p. 229 IGFA Collection

p. 234 Adrian Gray sportfishimages.com Photograph

p. 259 Chelsea Homesley Photograph

Index

About the Author

Ashley Oliphant has spent the last 15 years studying the works of Ernest Hemingway. She has a Ph.D. in 20th-Century American Literature from the University of North Carolina at Greensboro, and she has taught composition, literature, linguistics, and Hemingway seminars at the college level for more than a decade. She is currently on the English Department faculty at Pfeiffer University and serves as the Faculty Fellow for the Francis Center for Servant Leadership. Her 2007 dissertation, *Hemingway's Mixed Drinks: An Examination of the Varied Representation of Alcohol across the Author's Canon*, offered a formalistic approach to Hemingway's use of alcohol in his fiction and challenged many of the critics who have examined the topic using only a biographical approach. Oliphant is a longtime member of the Hemingway Society and has presented at two of the organization's international conferences. Teaching college students — seeing their imaginations ignited by great Hemingway books and guiding them through the complexities of literary modernism — is the most satisfying part of her job. Oliphant is married and has a five-year-old son and two mischievous cats. In her free time, she likes to float in her swimming pool, play a round of afternoon golf, tinker in her garden, and win concert tickets in radio contests.

For more books from Pineapple Press, visit our website at www.pineapplepress.com. There you can find author pages, discover new and upcoming books, and search our list for books that might interest you. Look for our weekly posts and give-aways, and be sure to sign up for our mailing list.

If you loved this book, look for these related books on our site:

Hemingway's Cats, Revised Cuba Edition by Carlene Brennan. Ernest Hemingway always had cats as companions, from the ones he adored as a child in Illinois and Michigan, to the more than 30 he had as an adult in Paris, Key West, Cuba, and Idaho. All are chronicled and most are pictured here, along with revelations about how they fit into the many twists and turns of his life and loves.

My Brother, Ernest Hemingway by Leicester Hemingway. First published in 1962, this updated edition includes a selection of letters from Ernest to his family never before published. If you want to know who Ernest Hemingway really was, read this book. (hb)

Hemingway's Key West Second Edition by Stuart McIver. A rousing, true-to-life portrait of Hemingway in Key West, Cuba, and Bimini during his heyday. Includes a two-hour walking tour of the author's favorite Key West haunts and a narrative of the places he frequented in Cuba.

Key West in History by Rodney and Loretta Carlisle. This photo-rich guide to things to see in Key West takes you through the nearly 200-year history of this unique town, era by era. Pirates, wreckers, Civil War sailors, Cuban rebels, presidents, writers and artists all left their mark on town, in homes and workplaces, museums and monuments.

The Florida Keys by John Viele. Three volumes include fascinating accounts of two centuries of island and maritime history in southernmost Florida, organized by topic. *Volume 1: A History of the Pioneers*; *Volume 2: True Stories of the Perilous Straits*; *Volume 3: The Wreckers*

The Houses of Key West by Alex Caemmerer. Color photos showcase an architectural treasure trove of houses built in the 19th century. Includes charming anecdotes about old Key West gleaned from interviews with descendants of the families who built houses there.

The Streets of Key West: A History Through Street Names by J. Wills Burke. Learn the history of the island at the end of the chain of the Florida Keys through the history of its street names. Discover how Simonton, Duval, Eaton, Whitehead, Southard, Truman, and all the others got their names.